Copyright © 2025 by Doni Glover
All rights reserved.

No part of this book may be reproduced, stored in a retrieval system,
or transmitted in any form or by any means—
electronic, mechanical,
photocopying, recording, or otherwise—without the prior written
permission of the publisher, except for brief
quotations used in reviews or scholarly works.

ISBN: **978-1-7373138-3-0**
Published by Bmorenews.com
Baltimore, MD

Printed in the United States of America

First Edition

For permissions, media inquiries, or bulk orders,
please contact doni@bmorenews.com.

BLACK BLUEPRINT: BALTIMORE TO BURKINA FASO

by
Doni Glover

DEDICATION

Dedicated to Robert "Bob" Ingram and Brother Naba'a Richard Muhammad. God bless their souls.

TABLE OF CONTENTS

Dedication	iv
Foreword, Ron Busby, Sr.	viii
Introduction	x
Chapter 1: Congressman Parren J. Mitchell	1
Chapter 2: Politics: Doc, Lillie, and William White	8
Chapter 3: The Birth of BMORENews: Betting on the Vision	13
Chapter 4: The Night That Changed Everything	18
Chapter 5: Media Power	21
Chapter 6: Know the Battlefield	29
Chapter 7: Black Business Is Political Power	41
Chapter 8: Greater Baltimore Politics	51
Chapter 9: We Do Have Power	60
Chapter 10: Partnering for Power—The U.S. Black Chambers	67

Chapter 11: Black Wall Street As A Mindset: Lessons From Dr. Michael Carter	76
Chapter 12: Black Wall Street Nation: From Harlem to the Heart of the South	89
Chapter 13: Brotherhood, Business & the BPM Way	101
Chapter 14: Fear, Power, and the Price of Reparations	106
Chapter 15: Legacy Over Lip Service	113
Chapter 16: Still in Civil Rights Mode	117
Chapter 17: We Know What Time It Is	123
Chapter 18: On My Mother: A Word on Wealth	129
Chapter 19: What's Next – Building the Future of Black Empowerment	134
Chapter 20: The Quiet Powerhouse: What the Funeral Business Taught Me About Black Economics	140
Chapter 21: A Journey to Africa: From Jordan to Addis Ababa	149
Chapter 22: BMORENEWS and the United Nations: Where It All Comes Together	151

Chapter 23: The Architect of New Africa — Ibrahim Traoré and the Road to Pan-African Sovereignty	158
Chapter 24: The Power We Carry: From Toussaint to Tomorrow	166
Chapter 25: Quiet Giants	171
Chapter 26: The Prince George's Power Surge	181
Chapter 27: The Power of Black Media Ownership: SUPPORT BLACK MEDIA!	192
Chapter 28: What I Would Say to My Younger Self	203
Chapter 29: Pass the Ball	207
Chapter 30: The Builders — Baltimore's Black Architects of Power	211
Chapter 31: The Grace We Must Give	230
Chapter 32: We Are the Blueprint	238
Afterword	248
Acknowledgements	251
About the Author	252

FOREWORD

In every movement, there are those who document the moment—and then there are those who help define it. Doni Glover does both.

Black Blueprint is more than a title—it's a testimony. It's a bold, unflinching record of a man who has spent decades on the frontlines of Black media, business, and community empowerment. Doni Glover is not just a journalist; he is a truth-teller, a platform builder, and a relentless advocate for Black economic power. Through *BMORENews, BlackUSA.News*, the Joe Manns Black Wall Street Awards, and his tireless community organizing, he has elevated thousands of voices that would otherwise go unheard.

This book captures the essence of Doni's mission: to shift the narrative, to shine the light on Black excellence, and to remind us that *we are our own blueprint*.

What you hold in your hands is part memoir, part manifesto. It's the culmination of lived experience—from West Baltimore to national platforms—and it speaks to a deeper truth: that

Black media and Black business are inseparable pillars of our progress. Doni understands, as I do, that economic justice is the unfinished business of the civil rights movement—and that storytelling is one of our most powerful tools for change.

I've had the honor of working alongside Doni as he's championed Black entrepreneurs not just in Maryland, but across the country. His work aligns with the mission of the U.S. Black Chambers—to build Black wealth, foster Black-owned businesses, and ensure that our communities are equipped for the future.

Black Blueprint isn't just Doni's story—it's a reflection of all of us who believe in legacy, ownership, and self-determination. Whether you're an entrepreneur, a student, a policymaker, or someone just trying to make a difference, this book offers wisdom, inspiration, and a path forward.

Read it. Reflect on it. Then get to work—because the blueprint is here.

— **Ron Busby, Sr.**
President & CEO
U.S. Black Chambers, Inc.
Washington, D.C.

INTRODUCTION

Black Blueprint

I was never meant to be a statistic.
I was raised to be a solution.

By the numbers, a Black boy from North Avenue surrounded by broken systems, flooded corners, and the long shadow of the crack era — wasn't expected to make it. Not as a journalist. Not as an entrepreneur. Not as an author. Not as a grandfather. And certainly not as a national advocate for Black business.

But I did — because my parents believed differently.

I was raised in a Black household rooted in faith, discipline, education, hard work, and service. My mother and father built a family business from the ground up. From that foundation, I was exposed to opportunities many of my peers didn't have.

We traveled — Florida to Canada. I had the church. I had music: a piano, an organ, even a trombone. I started piano lessons at age seven with Mr. Barton

LeBaron Bonds. My father even brought a trombonist to our home to sharpen my skills.

At Matthew A. Henson Elementary, I played in the school orchestra and led the morning broadcast. I joined the Boy Scouts. At eleven, I ran the largest *Afro* Newspaper route in West Baltimore — from Moreland and Baker to Edmondson and Warwick, home to Perkins Square Baptist Church. Then I'd re-up and cover the Sandtown leg, stretching all the way to Harlem Park.

That route taught me the fundamentals of business: customer service, collections, and consistency. I'll never forget my dad taking a quarter from his pocket and rapping it on a glass window. The lady came out in thirty seconds. He gave me that look — the kind that said, *"Now that's how it's done. Don't forget it."*

That same year, I played for the 1976 championship Mets in the James Mosher Baseball League — the oldest Black youth baseball league in America. I also played BNBL (Baltimore Neighborhood Basketball League) for Easterwood Rec. Earning that gray jersey was an urban dream. I was a stronger baseball player, but making the basketball team meant everything. Facing teams like Bentalou

Rec, locking in on defense — it gave you respect. I scored a couple buckets, sure, but the biggest honor was making the squad. That meant something in Baltimore. A shout-out to Ms. Eula Mae Williams and Ralph Durant in heaven, and to Ms. Jones-Bey: they were our community parents who helped save our lives.

Basketball and football moved faster than baseball, but baseball was—and still is—my first love. I lifted weights. I rode my bike across the city, even all the way to Randallstown. I trained in karate and boxing. I skated. I even studied Islamic teachings.

I didn't just survive my environment—I thrived in spite of it, and because of the people who poured into me. I was raised to believe I could do anything.

Former Maryland Chief Judge Robert Bell recently told me he was raised the same way. Judge Bell, who was classmates with Reginald F. Lewis, survived the concrete jungle too. So did Lewis. And they both persevered.

I was active. Focused. Busy living.

But the neighborhood I grew up in was under siege.

Drugs were everywhere—coke, dope, crack.

"Don't go around Warwick Avenue," my mother would warn. There was a bar on Warwick, just two blocks from our home. That's where the bad boys hung out.

By the time I turned eighteen—in 1983—the crack era was undeniable. Its low cost made it spread like wildfire. It destroyed lives, families, and futures.

I always remember Ronald Reagan, Col. Oliver North, and the Iran-Contra operation that helped fuel it. My community was devastated — abandoned homes, fires, mass exodus, murder rates through the roof. It wreaked hell on Baltimore and other Black cities across America.

And while Nancy Reagan told us to "just say no," today those same Black communities are overwhelmed by a new wave of addiction — this time, largely white.

The crack epidemic wasn't just a news headline in Baltimore. It was the backdrop of our daily lives. Liquor stores lined our blocks. Schools were crumbling. Whole generations were being lost.

Maryland still incarcerates Black people at one of the highest rates in the nation. We were being caged as early as we were being counted.

And yet, my parents planted something in me.
My village watered it.
And don't forget Grandma Flossie's prayers.

While others might've counted me out — and I almost did too — God didn't.

Having crossed many bridges, I know this much: With God, all things are possible.

Go ahead — tell me what I can't do.
I'll show you exactly what I was born to do.

This isn't just my story.
It's a blueprint.
A call to action.
A toolkit for Black empowerment — grounded in lived experience, real-world strategy, and an unshakable will to survive and thrive.

For nearly thirty years, I've worked at the intersection of business, media, and politics — building platforms, launching movements, and helping our people win.

Through the Joe Manns Black Wall Street Awards, we've honored nearly 3,000 Black entrepreneurs across nine U.S. cities.

Through *BMORENews.com, BlackUSA.News*, my Emmy-nominated podcast, and television platforms, we've amplified truth, confronted injustice, and spotlighted Black excellence.

They've called me a journalist. A businessman. A political whisperer. Even a troublemaker.

I'll take them all — because at my core, I am a strategist. And what our community needs now, more than ever, is strategy.

We've marched. We've built. We've endured.

But survival isn't the mission. Power is.
Real power — institutional, generational, and unapologetically Black.

For too long, others have told our stories — often through a lens that distorts our brilliance and magnifies our pain.

I elected to pick up the pen — and the mic, and the camera — to change that.

This book is about reclaiming our narrative and advancing our power.

It's about the policies, people, and movements that have carved paths to Black wealth and equity —

and the courage it takes to challenge the status quo along the way.

I'll never forget my first day of class with Professor Ronn Nichols at Coppin State. He sat us down, turned off the lights, and played *The Birth of a Nation* by D.W. Griffith. A silent film — yet loud with racism, lies, and propaganda.

Professor Nichols wanted us to understand the battlefield.
He wanted us to know the score.

He made it plain: as Black media professionals, we'd face choices — ones that would either uplift or degrade our people. The lesson? *Choose wisely.*

He showed us how Hollywood exported our humiliation — portraying us as frightened, foolish, wide-eyed caricatures — to justify our oppression.

That film was screened at the White House. President Woodrow Wilson, despite NAACP protests, praised it. It shaped how the world saw us. And it was designed to do exactly that.

That lesson never left me.
And that's why I do what I do.

Setting the Stage

Before we dive in, context matters.

Maryland—especially Baltimore—offers a unique political, economic, and cultural backdrop for Black America. Baltimore is a 9-to-1 Democratic stronghold in a state that leans 2-to-1 Democratic. Between Baltimore and Washington, D.C., a powerful demographic force emerges: 1.66 million African Americans. Statewide, Black residents make up nearly 30% of the population.

Economically, the picture is layered. In 2023, the median income for Black households in Maryland was $77,493—progress, yes, but still trailing the state's overall median of $101,652. Yet where disparities persist, so does determination.

As of 2024, Maryland is home to over 102,000 Black-owned businesses generating $6.8 billion in revenue. They represent 19.3% of all businesses statewide—second only to Georgia and the District of Columbia.

Rising within this economic engine is a force reshaping American business: the Black SheEO. Black women are the fastest-growing group of entrepreneurs in the U.S., and their momentum is palpable across Maryland—from Baltimore to Prince George's County and the D.C. metro area.

They are creating jobs, fueling innovation, and breaking through systemic barriers. More than just participating in the economy, Black women are redefining it—driven by vision, ownership, and community transformation.

Sharon Pinder has been honoring Maryland's Top 100 MBEs, including Black women entrepreneurs, for years, celebrating their leadership, innovation, and impact. Among those recognized are Doris McMillon of McMillon Communications, Inc., and Monica Mitchell of MERAssociates, LLC—two powerhouse women who exemplify the strength and vision driving Maryland's Black business community forward.

Politically, Maryland leads the nation in Black representation. As of 2025, the state boasts the largest Black legislative caucus in the country, with 64 members. The 2022 election of Governor Wes Moore marked Maryland as the only state led by a Black governor, followed in 2024 by Angela Alsobrooks making history as the first Black U.S. Senator from Maryland.

Nationally, Black America is a rising force. As of 2023, 48.3 million people in the U.S. identify as Black—about 14.4% of the population—with a collective buying power of $1.98 trillion. If that were its own economy, it would rank around the 10th largest in the world, rivaling nations like Brazil, Canada, and South Korea. This economic power drives entrepreneurship, shapes culture, and influences politics.

This is the landscape: engaged, resilient, economically powerful, and globally connected. A place of contrast and complexity—but also of boundless potential.

And within this fertile ground, our story begins to unfold.

Today, Africa is reclaiming its sovereignty. For too long, despite supplying the Global North with cobalt, platinum, gold, and diamonds, African nations have remained burdened by debt and dependence. But now, countries like Burkina Faso, Niger, and Mali are charting new paths toward self-determination.

This is our moment.

Rooted in legacy. Fueled by data. Backed by numbers they can't ignore.

From the corners of Baltimore to the streets of Ouagadougou, the blueprint is being written.

Page by page. Brick by brick.

And this is where the blueprint begins.

CHAPTER 1

CONGRESSMAN PARREN J. MITCHELL

"This is quite a game, politics. There are no permanent enemies, and no permanent friends, only permanent interests." – William Clay

This powerful landscape of political influence, economic strength, and cultural resilience in Maryland did not emerge overnight. It was shaped by visionaries and disruptors who paved the way—leaders who understood that building power required both grit and strategy. At the forefront of this legacy stands Congressman Parren J. Mitchell, Maryland's first Black Congressman and one of the most formidable architects of Black economic and political empowerment in the state.

Mitchell's journey began with a historic challenge to segregation: in 1950, with support from the Baltimore Branch of the NAACP, he sued the then-segregated University of Maryland for admission to its graduate school—and won. When he graduated, he became the first African American to do so from that institution. This victory was more than personal; it was a foundational step toward dismantling institutional barriers.

Throughout his career, Mitchell built on that momentum by crafting policies that institutionalized equity and opportunity. His leadership was marked by groundbreaking achievements such as the Minority Enterprise Act (1976–77), which expanded the Small Business Administration's capacity to serve Black entrepreneurs; the 10% Set-Aside Amendment (1977), mandating that governments using federal funds allocate at least 10% to minority-owned firms; and the Highway Bill Amendment (1982), which provided protections for disadvantaged business owners.

Mitchell also battled Reagan-era rollbacks and founded the Minority Business Legal Defense and Education Fund to protect these hard-won gains. He didn't just open doors—he built lasting frameworks for Black economic and political power. His legacy of intentional leadership and unwavering determination laid the blueprint that continues to shape Maryland's progress today. And he was not alone.

Giants like **Doug Sands, Robert Lee Clay, Robert Dashiell, Arnold Jolivet, Hank Arrington, Wilbert Wilson, Wayne Frazier, Rev. Chet Williams**, and **Stanley Tucker** weren't just advocates—they were, and some still are, architects of Black economic infrastructure in Maryland and beyond.

Wayne Curry, former Prince George's County Executive, and **Raymond V. Haysbert, Sr.**, the "Dean of Business," took the torch further — blending political power with economic uplift. They proved that Black political capital could build real, sustained wealth.

And of course, **Marion Barry**, D.C.'s "Mayor-for-Life," redefined political leadership. Known first as "the jobs man," Barry used the mayor's office to hire and empower Black residents, reshaping D.C. and influencing Prince George's County's rise as the wealthiest majority-Black county in America. As Barry once told me about an upcoming Baltimore election: *"If they stop listening, vote the bums out."* I never forgot that. Because I've seen how **every vote** — literally every single one — matters.

In fact, **Kweisi Mfume** once won by just six votes. **Johnny Olszewski**, when elected Baltimore County

Executive, won by only 17 ballots—he was the longshot among three key contenders. That's strategy. That's power. That's the point.

And sometimes, strategy means defying party lines.

In the early 2000s, another member of the Mitchell Family would arise. When **State Senator Clarence Mitchell IV**, a Black Democrat, endorsed Republican **Bob Ehrlich** for governor — the political world was stunned. But this wasn't about party. It was about power. Black voters were being ignored, so Mitchell made a strategic move. Ehrlich, along with his running mate **Michael Steele**, brought Black issues to the forefront.

The results?

1. **MBE** became a cabinet-level priority.

2. Maryland's **HBCUs** received long-overdue investment.

3. **Sharon Pinder** became Special Secretary for Minority Affairs, a post that was elevated to a cabinet position.

4. The **Small Business Reserve Program** was born.

5. Black businesses gained more access to business opportunities.

This wasn't just a change in administration — it was a shift in posture. From neglected to negotiated. From begging to bargaining.

This book is about how power really works—and how we build it. Not just through voting, but through organizing. Not just through protest, but through preparation. Not just with hope, but with strategy. Sometimes, it's less about who you back and more about who you refuse to.

This blueprint is for those ready to do more than survive. It's for storytellers, entrepreneurs, disruptors, and builders. It's for anyone who's been made to feel invisible, disposable, or done.

If you've ever doubted your value, your voice, or your vision — let this be your reminder to stand tall. Because we are not invisible. We are not disposable. And we are far from done. We stand on the broad shoulders of our ancestors, anointed with their wisdom to navigate what's to come. They survived so that we might live, and live abundantly.

Our path forward takes more than hope — it demands action. And that action starts with understanding that politics isn't some far-off spectacle. I often hear, "I'm not into politics." But here's the truth: politics is into you. It shapes everything — who gets what, when, and where. And that "what" often means access to limited resources and real opportunities. Politics is personal. It's local. It's where power is negotiated — and where change begins.

Let me tell you about the people who showed me how this game works — how politics chose me, shaped me, and still guides me today.

Closing Reflection

Congressman Parren J. Mitchell and the giants who stood alongside him laid a foundation not just of political wins, but of enduring Black economic and political power in Maryland. Their grit, strategy, and vision remind us that power isn't given — it's built with intentionality and courage.

This legacy teaches us that true influence comes from understanding the game, sometimes playing outside party lines, and always putting community first. It's a blueprint for how to move from invisibility to impact, from surviving to thriving.

As we carry this story forward, let it be clear: our future is shaped by those who organize, strategize, and refuse to be sidelined. Politics is not a distant game — it is the battleground for our economic opportunity and dignity.

Hence, stand tall. Speak with purpose. And remember — we are seen, we matter, and we are just getting started. The work goes on, and the power is ours to seize.

CHAPTER 2

POLITICS: DOC, LILLIE, AND WILLIAM WHITE

I've spent much of my life as vice-president — literally. It started in elementary school, and it still holds true today as I serve as Vice-President of the Sandtown-Winchester Community Collective. I didn't choose politics; it chose me early. And honestly, I never resisted. There's something about leadership — even from the second seat — that always felt familiar.

Some of my earliest memories are political. I remember being a child standing beside my father at a fundraiser for Congressman Parren J. Mitchell at Mondawmin Mall. That day, I believe I met Arthur Murphy, too. He was Billy Murphy's younger brother. I was fascinated by the energy, the suits, the way grown men and women wielded words and power. I soaked it up. At home, I'd watch *Square Off* on WJZ-TV like other kids watched cartoons. I can still picture Northwestern High School Principal Boyse Mosley trading jabs with Georgia Goslee, Madeline Murphy, and St.

George Crosse. Politics was theater — but it was real, and it mattered.

My father, Doc Glover, made sure I knew what was going on in the world. He insisted I be informed. He'd give me editorials to read and had me listen to Carl T. Rowan and Paul Harvey do commentaries on the radio. Born in the wake of Malcolm X's assassination and crawling through East Baltimore while the flames of the '68 riots still smoldered, I didn't just witness history — I inherited it. Even as a kid, I could feel the angst that adults were experiencing with racial hatred in this country. Maybe politics has always been my calling. All I know is that I'd collect campaign signs like baseball cards. I'll never forget the bold election signs of A. Dwight Pettit for State's Attorney — something about them always grabbed me.

One day, just before I graduated from Dunbar High School, my mother, Lillie Juanita Glover, grabbed me by the hand and walked me out of our house on Moreland Avenue. We strolled down to Baker Street and made a left across the alley to the second house — the home of Senator Troy Brailey. I didn't fully understand the weight of that visit at the time, but she was walking me into a new season. Senator

Brailey wasn't just a neighbor; he was a Baltimore legend — a former labor organizer who helped lead the 1963 March on Washington, a civil rights trailblazer, and one of the most trusted Black legislators in Annapolis. His house had been a meeting ground for giants: Willie Mays, Bayard Rustin, Jackie Robinson, A. Philip Randolph. And that day, it became a launching pad for me. I walked out with a Senatorial Scholarship that helped me get to college. That moment wasn't about luck — it was about preparation, proximity, and a mother who believed access to power wasn't optional. It was necessary. Because when someone like Senator Brailey opens a door, it's not just for one person — it's for the people coming behind you.

Politics ran in both my parents' blood. I learned that they used to host political gatherings in East Baltimore. These weren't just parties — they were strategy sessions. That legacy didn't skip a generation. I got it honest.

In 1997, my elementary school classmate, William Fitzgerald White, pulled me deeper into the game. He was a natural political strategist, and he convinced me to run for the Democratic State Central Committee in the 44th District. I ran in 1998 and came in sixth — just one spot shy of victory. They only seated five. It stung, but what I gained was far more valuable than a title: I got a front-row seat to grassroots politics. That race became my political bootcamp. I learned how campaigns work — the messaging, the strategy, the handshakes, and the hard truths.

Losing that race wasn't the end — it was the education. Because in politics, as in life, sometimes you learn more in the loss than in the win.

Reflection: The Power is Local

What I learned from Doc, Lillie, and William White is this: **politics isn't something you watch — it's something you do.** And it's more than pulling a lever. Real power isn't just in Washington, D.C. — it's in the school board meetings, community associations, campaign offices, and neighborhood living rooms where decisions are made that shape our everyday lives. That's why the teachers knew my father's name when he would spot-check me in elementary school.

We can't afford to sit out. Every piece of progress in our community — from school funding to police reform to business grants — is influenced by someone at a table. **If we're not at the table, we're likely on the menu.**

We don't all have to run for office. But we do have to stay engaged. We have to contribute to campaigns. Knock doors. Put up signs. Host forums. It's certainly more than just voting. Teach our kids how power works. Because the work of rebuilding Black Wall Street doesn't start in the White House — it starts right where you are.

Just like my mama knew.

And I stayed in it.

Not politics in the traditional sense — but the kind that lives in headlines, camera lenses, and community voices. I realized early on that media *is* power. If politics determines the rules, then media shapes the narrative. And in 2002, I decided to control the narrative.

and came in sixth — just one spot shy of victory. They only seated five. It stung, but what I gained was far more valuable than a title: I got a front-row seat to grassroots politics. That race became my political bootcamp. I learned how campaigns work — the messaging, the strategy, the handshakes, and the hard truths.

Losing that race wasn't the end — it was the education. Because in politics, as in life, sometimes you learn more in the loss than in the win.

Reflection: The Power is Local

What I learned from Doc, Lillie, and William White is this: **politics isn't something you watch — it's something you do.** And it's more than pulling a lever. Real power isn't just in Washington, D.C. — it's in the school board meetings, community associations, campaign offices, and neighborhood living rooms where decisions are made that shape our everyday lives. That's why the teachers knew my father's name when he would spot-check me in elementary school.

We can't afford to sit out. Every piece of progress in our community — from school funding to police reform to business grants — is influenced by someone at a table. **If we're not at the table, we're likely on the menu.**

We don't all have to run for office. But we do have to stay engaged. We have to contribute to campaigns. Knock doors. Put up signs. Host forums. It's certainly more than just voting. Teach our kids how power works. Because the work of rebuilding Black Wall Street doesn't start in the White House — it starts right where you are.

Just like my mama knew.

And I stayed in it.

Not politics in the traditional sense — but the kind that lives in headlines, camera lenses, and community voices. I realized early on that media *is* power. If politics determines the rules, then media shapes the narrative. And in 2002, I decided to control the narrative.

CHAPTER 3

THE BIRTH OF BMORENEWS: BETTING ON THE VISION

"If God gives you the vision, He'll give you the provision."

In 2002, I took a leap of faith.

After my time at Empower Baltimore Management Corporation came to an end, I received a $16,000 severance check. I could've played it safe. Paid some bills. Waited on the next job. But instead, I bet it all—on me.

With that check, I paid off my house and launched **BMORENews.com**, a platform built to tell our stories, unfiltered. Alongside it, I started **DMGlobal**, my PR and marketing firm. It was more than a business decision—it was a calling rooted in both purpose and persistence.

At the time, Republican voices were still largely unwelcome in Black media spaces. And for good reason. Though once the party of Lincoln, by the

2000s the GOP had become linked with Reaganomics, Iran-Contra, and a string of policies that neglected urban America. Black legacy outlets like *The Afro* carried a justified skepticism. Still, something in the air felt different in 2002. I wanted to challenge narratives, not just repeat them. I didn't fit neatly in anyone's box—and I liked it that way.

Writing was always my strength. But I'd already earned stripes in radio and television by then. Still, print journalism gave me my first real credibility.

It started with *The Sandtown-Winchester Viewpoint*, my neighborhood newspaper. I served as editor and co-editor from 1994 to 2001. Looking back, that was my true professional start. Month after month, we published 48-page issues and delivered them door to door. It wasn't glamorous, but it was real. I got to know the people—really know them. I told their stories with dignity. Even now, folks still come up to me and say, *"You wrote about my grandmother,"* or, *"You did a piece on my shop."* And I remember them, too. Every story mattered—because every person did.

My TV break came through my classmate Cassandra Vaughn Claxton, a producer at WBAL-

TV 11 and the daughter of the great Dr. A.C.D. Vaughn. She reported to her godmother, the one and only **Wanda Draper**, who had once produced shows for the legendary **Kweisi Mfume**. Cassandra brought me in to do political commentary—and that door stayed open for nearly a decade. I even got prime-time air at the news desk, sitting alongside icons like **Frank D. Felipo** and **Levy Rabinowitz**. For a young Black man from West Baltimore, that wasn't just exposure—it was elevation.

My voice in radio began in 1999 through my work with the Empowerment Zone. That led to a weekly show on **WOLB 1010 AM**, part of **Radio One Baltimore**. When the contract ended, I kept going independently. Thanks to a generous investment by **Joe Haskins** of **Harbor Bank of Maryland**, I launched a second show—one he personally funded for nearly four years.

Over 21 years, I hosted the **longest-running customized news talk show** in Radio One history. My guests were entrepreneurs, returning citizens, scholars, judges, artists—you name it. The formula was simple: give people a platform. Make them visible. Let them be heard.

I didn't have corporate backing or a network. I had a story, a mic, and a commitment to my people. That was enough to build something that's still standing today.

Reflection

Looking back, that $16,000 wasn't just severance—it was seed money. A divine test of faith. I didn't have a blueprint. I didn't have a safety net. All I had was conviction—that I had something to say, and that my community needed to hear it.

Every article I wrote, every interview I recorded, every late night spent editing videos, designing graphics, formatting websites—it was all an act of service. I built platforms because too few were telling our truth. And I kept building, because I realized something fundamental: when we own the mic, we control the message. That's the power of purpose. That's the power of betting on yourself.

And it didn't take long before that purpose intersected with politics.

There are a few words from my father that still ring in my ears today—and they're part of what inspire me to keep doing the Joe Manns Black Wall Street Awards. He told me, "Doni, get out there and try.

If you do that, somebody might see you. They might even help you. But you'll never know if you never try." I did exactly that. And, lo and behold, someone did help me.

God rest his soul—Julian Moore gave *BMORENews* an immediate lift, helping us get into video reporting at a time when hardly anyone in our space was doing it. My 25-year colleague, Marc Clarke, regularly tells how I would pop-up with my digital camera, cover a story, and have the video loaded before the 5 pm newscast.

And then there was this gem from Pops. When I complained about not getting any business, he looked at me and said, "Beat your drum!"

I went back two weeks later, still frustrated, and told him, "Doc, I'm beating my drum, but no one's listening." Without missing a beat, he said, "Beat your drum harder!"

Those words are etched in me. They became my rhythm. My resilience. My blueprint.

CHAPTER 4

THE NIGHT THAT CHANGED EVERYTHING

We brought in Congressman Bob Ehrlich to speak at the Harambee Dinner Club at Britton's on North Howard Street. But I wasn't about to let it become a campaign stop. So, I called in a heavyweight: Attorney and former judge William "Billy" Murphy, Jr.

Billy didn't come to play. He came to deliver. MIT-educated, unapologetically Black, and fearless in any room, he walked in like a storm and lit the place up. No soft gloves. No code-switching. Just raw truth and brilliance. Unfiltered.

That night, he reminded everyone in the room—and me most of all—that authenticity is power. And power never asks for permission.

What started as a dinner turned into a political flashpoint. Conversations sparked that evening rippled out into something bigger. By November 2002, Bob Ehrlich was elected Governor of Maryland. But the history-maker? Michael S.

Steele—sworn in as the first Black person ever elected to statewide office in Maryland.

On Election Day, ten-foot-tall Steele posters stood outside polling places in Black communities across the state. Leading that ground game was Senator Clarence Mitchell IV—C4. He didn't just back the ticket—he put his name, his legacy, and his future on the line to send a message: Black voters were nobody's property.

That moment wasn't about party—it was about power. It was about strategy. And it was about Black Marylanders taking the pen back and writing ourselves into the narrative.

Closing Reflection

That night at Britton's wasn't just another dinner— it was a turning point. Billy Murphy's unfiltered truth reminded us all that authenticity is the foundation of real power. Power doesn't ask for permission; it demands to be recognized.

What unfolded wasn't about party politics. It was about Black Marylanders reclaiming their voice and their influence. From the bold leadership of Michael Steele to Clarence Mitchell IV's fearless ground game, we showed that Black voters are not pawns—they are power players.

This moment was a vivid example of how strategy, courage, and unity can rewrite history. It proved that when we refuse to be sidelined, when we bring our full selves to the table, we don't just participate in democracy—we transform it.

The night that changed everything reminds us: the pen is in our hands. The story is ours to write. And when we stand authentically, unapologetically, we move mountains.

CHAPTER 5

MEDIA POWER

Before, television controlled the mind. Today, social media dominates it. We must own our voices—especially the right voices—not rent them.

Malcolm X said it best: "The media is the most powerful entity on earth. It can make the innocent look guilty and the guilty look innocent." That quote has never left me. I've seen it play out over and over again.

I never thought I'd share this publicly, but here it is:
If you want to make a real impact in your community, you must have a communications arm. Period.

Why? Because if you're not telling your own story, someone else is—and trust me, it will never be the same. No one can represent your truth like you can.

Take it from me. I'm the founder of *BMORENews.com*, and for more than two decades, I've been pushing out our stories—stories of struggle, triumph, and transformation. It's personal. It's powerful. And it's strategic.

Being visible means being proactive. It also means we have to counterpunch the gibberish pushed by certain mainstream outlets—those that spotlight Black squeegee kids on Baltimore corners while saying nothing about the non-Black homeless addicts who've flooded our communities since the 2015 Freddie Gray Unrest and the Consent Decree that followed.

Let me give you a real-life example. I graduated from Paul Laurence Dunbar Community High School in historic East Baltimore—the same year our basketball team, led by Reggie Williams and Tyrone "Muggsy" Bogues, won the national championship. That moment was pure Poet Pride, written in the hearts of everyone who lived it.

Years later, an author from Brooklyn wrote a book about that team. Some of the guys were excited—but me? Not so much. I don't care how well-written the book was. If you weren't there, you can't tell it like we can. No outsider can feel what we felt, can capture what it meant. We have to be the ones to write our own books.

That same principle applies everywhere. Just like we can create national dance crazes or viral challenges, we must channel that same creative energy into preserving our histories—our truths—on all platforms. And yes, I believe everyone should write a book. It's easier than you think. And if you want to change your neighborhood, your city—**start by building your own website.** It's never been more affordable.

Here's why it matters: a website—especially one with a video component and active social media—is a game-changer. Politicians crave visibility. So do businesses. If your platform highlights their work, they will pay attention. And when campaign season rolls around, they'll spend money to be seen.

Let me be real, though: if all you do is slam politicians, don't expect them to advertise with you. Nobody wants to pay for a beatdown. But if your coverage is fair—if you call them out when necessary and credit them when it's due—they'll respect you. Balance is key.

Next, build an email list. A strong newsletter helps reinforce your posts. If you're a one-person team, aim for two to three updates a week. Consistency builds trust and visibility.

Eventually, you'll need a team. Learn how to delegate. Pay people for their time. As Eddie Brown of Brown Capital Management once said, *you've got to offer the best compensation package in the region.* **That takes sponsorships and advertisers.** And people do business with people they like—plain and simple.

Sometimes, you'll lose business through no fault of your own. A contact retires, someone new steps in, and the checks stop coming. It happens. Don't panic—just keep building. Find your next opportunity. I believe firmly: if God brought you to it, He'll bring you through it. When one door closes, another opens. And if you stay ready, you don't have to get ready.

For me, being ready means I keep two phones on me—an Android and an iPhone. I shoot video and take photos on the fly. I'm no tech whiz, but I get the job done. When I turned 55, T-Mobile offered me a second phone on the cheap. I jumped on it. Now I've got options—two lenses to capture the truth.

But we also have to talk about the more subtle media messaging—the kind that doesn't make headlines, but shapes minds. Mainstream platforms have a long history of making Black things seem bad. Blackballed. Blackeye. Black heart. Black out. Black cat. Black magic. Black hole. Blacklisted. Blackmail. Black Friday. Black sheep. Black site. That includes how we talk, how we walk, how we parent—and how we wear our hair.

Too often, Black women are portrayed wearing weaves or wigs, while natural styles—afros, coils, twists, braids—rarely make the screen. The subliminal message? That natural isn't good enough. And when media keeps reinforcing that image, it shapes what's seen as "professional," "beautiful," or "acceptable."

That's not vanity—it's survival in a system that rewards conformity. Many of our sisters spend hundreds of dollars each month on hair products, often manufactured in South Korea—not because they lack pride, but because they've been pressured by a lie.

That's media influence. That's image warfare. And it's costing us—in confidence, in dollars, and in identity.

The global hair weave and extension industry is booming. In 2023, it was valued at over $8 billion and is projected to approach $12 billion by 2029. North America holds the largest market share, while the Asia-Pacific region is growing fastest.

That's the power of media. That's the danger of silence. And that's why we have to speak—not just loudly, but consistently. Because media isn't neutral. It's either working for us or against us. And if we don't control the narrative, we'll keep being controlled by it.

Bottom line? If you care about your community, build a news outlet. It's more doable than you think. After 23 years in this game doing it for myself, I've learned a few things. And I'm open to consulting anyone who wants to get started.

Telling our own stories isn't just important—it's necessary. Mainstream media will never cover us like we can. Their perspective is often shaped by whiteness, which means our realities—the full spectrum of Black life—get overlooked or distorted.

It's time to change that.
It's time to own our power.
It's time to tell our truth.

Telling our truth isn't just about media—it's about power. And in America, real power moves through politics. If we want better schools, safer streets, and true justice, we need to understand how the political game is played. And that means knowing the battlefield.

Closing Reflection

Media isn't just about storytelling—it's about shaping reality, influencing minds, and wielding power. As Malcolm X warned, whoever controls the narrative controls the truth. For too long, Black stories have been filtered through lenses that don't fully see or understand us. That changes when we take control of our voices and our platforms.

Building a media presence—whether through a website, newsletter, social media, or video channel—is more than a creative outlet; it's a strategic act of empowerment. By telling our own stories, we reclaim our history, honor our struggles, and celebrate our victories. We carve out space for authentic representation—something no outsider can imitate—especially when we leverage cross-promotion to amplify our reach.

But this work requires dedication, balance, and a willingness to adapt. It's about building trust with your audience, engaging political leaders without losing integrity, and staying ready for the challenges that come with growth.

Owning our media power means owning our political power. Without controlling the narrative, we surrender influence. And without influence, we forfeit the chance to demand better schools, safer neighborhoods, and equitable justice.

So, if you care about your community—if you want to see real change—start here. Build your platform. Tell your truth. Because in today's world, media is the battlefield, and our voices must be heard loud and clear.

It's time to intentionally and unapologetically own our power. And yes, it can be profitable. Years ago, media entrepreneur Keith Clinkscales said that the three paths to wealth are banking, real estate, and media. I chose—and still choose—media first. I believe it's my purpose. It's what drives my peace.

Clinkscales is best known as the former CEO of REVOLT Media & TV and Vanguarde Media, Inc. Today, he leads KTC Ventures, continuing his mission to empower through media.

CHAPTER 6

KNOW THE BATTLEFIELD

"The supreme art of war is to subdue the enemy without fighting." —Sun Tzu

Sun Tzu, the ancient master strategist, teaches that the true victory in war is achieved not through prolonged fighting or destruction, but by understanding the battlefield well enough to win without ever engaging in battle. He warns that war is costly—draining resources, morale, and the very lifeblood of a nation. Prolonged conflict dulls weapons, exhausts soldiers, and empties treasuries, leaving a people vulnerable to rivals and ruin. The wise leader moves swiftly and decisively, for victory depends not on length of campaign but on timing, resourcefulness, and the ability to exploit the enemy's weaknesses. Above all, knowing both yourself and your enemy is the surest path to triumph.

In the American political arena, especially for Black leaders, Sun Tzu's lessons on terrain and timing are as relevant today as ever. The political landscape is uniquely treacherous—shaped by race, money, power, and unseen gatekeepers. Winning this battle requires more than ambition; it demands deep intelligence, loyalty, and an unshakable understanding of the battlefield before stepping onto it. Politics is not about fairness—it's about access. Money opens doors; race influences the journey; power often lurks behind closed doors. Without recognizing this reality, a leader risks becoming a pawn in someone else's game.

True survival in this arena depends on mastering the unwritten rules: building trust that cannot be bought, cultivating intelligence that anticipates betrayal, and assembling a brain trust rather than a fan club. Leaders must own their narrative and serve their people with a clarity of purpose that becomes their greatest armor. The battles are as much about controlling information and timing as they are about strategy and strength—just as Sun Tzu prescribed long ago.

Maryland's political evolution demonstrates this clearly—where loyalty without reward gave way to demands for real influence. The old playbook of tokenism and backroom deals no longer holds sway. Black political power has learned to wield itself strategically, shaping outcomes not by force alone but by mastering the terrain, timing the strike, and understanding the art of political warfare.

The Future Is Ours—If We Claim It
Black Marylanders make up nearly 30% of the population. We are entrepreneurs, homeowners, veterans, educators, artists, and organizers. We are the pulse of this state.

And we're no longer satisfied with being seen—we demand to be heard.
This moment calls for transparency. For accountability. For power used wisely and unapologetically.

We are not waiting to be invited to the table. We are bringing our own chairs, our own agendas—and building our own institutions.

Howard "Pete" Rawlings: The Quiet Architect of Power
In the hardball world of Annapolis politics, one man stood out with unmatched clarity and conviction: Delegate Howard "Pete" Rawlings.

As Chair of the House Appropriations Committee, Pete didn't just hold a title—he wielded real power. A mathematician by training, his intellect was razor-sharp. He had a rare ability to convert political leverage into tangible results for those who needed it most.

Pete was no showboat. He was disciplined, deliberate, and deeply strategic. And he made sure that West Baltimore—and Black Maryland—was never overlooked. To a young journalist like me, Pete wasn't just a legislator; he was a mentor and a living embodiment of Black excellence in leadership. His legacy lives on through his daughter, Stephanie Rawlings-Blake, former Mayor of Baltimore.

Pete understood the true nature of politics: it decides who gets what, when, and where. And he ensured we were at the table—not left on the menu.

Prince George's County: Where Black Power Got Wealthy

To understand the momentum of Black political power in Maryland in the early 2000s, you had to understand Prince George's County.

Under the leadership of D.C.'s Marion Barry and Prince George's own Wayne Curry, the county rose to become the wealthiest majority-Black jurisdiction in America.

I'll never forget the day my friend, entrepreneur William Hopson, brought me to a Terry McAuliffe fundraiser in Woodmoor. Million-dollar homes. A Black-owned golf course. A neighborhood steeped in wealth, elegance, and political sophistication. Baltimore had Black people. Prince George's had Black power—with disposable income.

From that moment on, I was hooked. I started hosting networking events from north to south across the county. I met Black professionals with yachts, horse stables, and deep political savvy. These weren't nouveau riche elites. These were seasoned players who understood the landscape—and how to move within it.

And I knew: if Baltimore's Black voting bloc ever aligned with Prince George's? It'd be game over. That's not just influence—that's a movement.

A Broader Vision: Beyond Baltimore, Into the DMV

That wealth and influence don't stop at county

lines—they ripple throughout the DMV region, amplifying Black political power in new ways.

Being from Baltimore carries weight in Annapolis. But understanding the D.C./Prince George's dynamic? That gives you a whole other level of clout.

One of *BMORENews.com's* greatest strengths has always been its regional reach—from Baltimore to the entire DMV. That's how I got to interview icons like Marion Barry, how I developed a working relationship with Wayne Curry, and how I built bridges across jurisdictions and generations.

Both men believed in Black media. They recognized our role in the ecosystem. And their belief still fuels me today.

That's the engine behind everything I do: the unwavering conviction that Black voices matter.

Gatekeepers and the Black Political Paradox
Every institution—politics, business, media—has gatekeepers.

Let me be honest: I don't like them.

Especially when they look like me. Especially when they're Black and Democratic.
Where's the spirit of Harriet Tubman? Would Bea Gaddy have slammed the door shut? Would Kenny Harris or Raymond Haysbert have hoarded access? Never.

I was raised with a simple principle: if God puts you in a position to help, then help. No ego. No games. And if you can't help, at least don't harm.

"To whom much is given, much is required."

Too many folks get a taste of power and guard the gate like it's their inheritance. They forget who helped them rise. That's not leadership. That's cowardice.

But amidst gatekeepers who hoard access, there are also those who embody true leadership.

I think of Jerome Stephens, who worked for Senator Ben Cardin. I supported Kweisi Mfume in that race, but Jerome still took my calls. That's integrity. That's leadership.

Unfortunately, for every Jerome, there are ten others who treat access like a private club. That mindset is toxic. And thank God Harriet Tubman wasn't like them.

As Kendrick said: "They not like us."

But I've met the real ones—Tommie Broadwater, Wayne Curry, Billy Murphy. Men who didn't hoard power. They shared it. Sometimes all it took was a phone call or a kind word. And that one gesture could change a life.

That's how you build movements. That's how you strengthen a people.
Flaws and all, I'll say it plainly: I'll bet on Black every time.

Money: The Oxygen of Politics
This is why I've never run for office.

Raising money? Not for a title. If I'm fundraising, it's for BMORENews.com—not a campaign.

My job is to stay independent—close enough to influence, far enough to tell the truth.

Politics is war. And I made a promise: no campaign until I can fund it myself. If I go to battle, I bring my own armor.

You've got to be all in. And if you're not? Sit it out.

Look at Wes Moore. Barack Obama. They built war chests, built their bases, moved with purpose—and when the moment came, they rolled with assassins. Experts. Strategists.

Executioners.

Even William Donald Schaefer understood that. He was known for surrounding himself with people smarter than himself.

And let's be clear: you must raise money.

Sheila Dixon? One of the best fundraisers I've ever seen. Three hours a day, every day. Laser-focused. That's what it takes.

If you can't raise money, you're not ready. Sit down. And study.

A young man once called me about running for

office. Didn't know the incumbents.

Didn't know the district. That's political malpractice. It's not just who you know, but what you know about who you know; in particular, the relationships. Getting into a race blind of this is definitely not advisable.

Take Baltimore County's 10th District—Randallstown. You better talk to Delores Kelley. She's retired, but still powerful. Speaker Adrienne Jones? A force. Senator Ben Brooks? Learning from both. Council Chair Julian Jones? A likely candidate for County Executive; he'd be the first Black to hold that seat if he wins.

Know the players. Know the history. Know the game.

Closing Reflection: Real Leaders Open Doors

The stakes are high. The ground is shifting. But this remains true:
Real leaders open doors. They don't block them.

The world already erects enough barriers to keep us out—we don't need to build our own. Instead, let's build **bridges**. Let's build **movements**. Let's build **power**.

Baltimore is unapologetically political. Here, power doesn't always announce itself—but it always shows up.
As a wise friend once put it: *"Rich yells. Wealth whispers."*

The real gatekeepers don't host press conferences or pose for selfies with power.
They move pieces. They move the city.

Baltimore politics is a full-contact sport. Honestly, it might be easier to win the Governor's mansion than the Mayor's seat in this town.
And let's be clear: **Elections don't make leaders— leaders make elections.**
They organize. Strategize. Fund. And when necessary, they disrupt.
They understand the difference between **clout** and **control**.
Because real power lives in boardrooms—not just behind microphones.

This city's political DNA was shaped by its tribes— Germans, Poles, Irish, Jews—and now, a growing

Latino presence. Each carved out its own political machine. The old Democratic clubs may have faded, but new power players are rising. And the rules? They're being rewritten as we speak.

One thing is certain: Political power no longer lives only in City Hall or party headquarters.
Today, it thrives where **money meets influence—** Where **Black business becomes Black political power.**

So let's make sure we're not just watching history unfold.
Let's make sure **we're the ones holding the pen.**

CHAPTER 7

BLACK BUSINESS IS POLITICAL POWER

Black business *is* political. Always has been. Economic power becomes political power. Those who control capital often control policy.

That's why Black business groups aren't just networking hubs—they're engines of influence.

Baltimore has a rich tradition of Black entrepreneurship. Institutions like the Presidents' Roundtable and the Greater Baltimore Black Chamber of Commerce have long shaped not just wealth, but policy.

Under Devin Jackson, the Chamber is showing what a modern, 21st-century Black business ecosystem looks like.

Across Maryland—from Prince George's to Southern Maryland—Black chambers are stepping into the arena as full policy influencers, not just service providers.

Wayne Frazier and the Maryland-Washington Minority Companies Association are continuing the legacy of Arnold Jolivet. Every May, his Martin's West breakfast draws the region's most powerful players.

The Maryland Minority Contractors Association, now led by former Mayor Sheila Dixon, is also flexing new political muscle. Her work cutting through red tape for Black businesses is unmatched.

These groups aren't optional—they're essential. And now, elected officials know they can't ignore them.

Strong Black business institutions make it *easier* to elect Black leaders—and *harder* for them to be overlooked.

We've seen this work before. In the '60s and '70s, it was the preacher, the lawyer, the entrepreneur, the activist, the politician—each playing their part with purpose. That unity opened doors for the first generation of Black elected officials.

Then came integration, a double-edged sword. Doors to opportunity opened, but with them came fragmentation. Many moved away—from West

Baltimore to Woodlawn, Randallstown, Owings Mills—scattered and dispersed.

Today, those very neighborhoods are flipping. Homes once sold for $19,000 now fetch $200,000 or more. Yet, too often, we're not the ones holding the deeds or controlling the future of these communities.

This is where Marcus Garvey's vision becomes crucial. Garvey understood that unity is not about feelings or rhetoric—it's about structure, discipline, and relentless execution. It means putting ego aside and committing fully to the mission.

Not everyone will get it right away. That's okay. But we can't slow down for those still catching up.

We've seen the blueprint.

For years, a quiet but powerful force shaped Baltimore's political landscape: the Goon Squad—a strategic alliance of Morgan State professors and Black clergy. They weren't flashy or loud; they understood the power of patience and playing the long game.

Back in the '70s and '80s, the Black church was the heart of political strength and community mobilization. Today, as many congregations have moved to the suburbs, so too has much of that political power shifted alongside them.

That's why I write so much about Liberty Road and Northwest Baltimore County. It's home to one of the most resource-rich, educated, and untapped Black voting blocs in Maryland.

The power is there. They just have to *own* it.

The Blueprint That Still Works

Republicans cracked the code in Maryland.

Robert Ehrlich picked Michael Steele—who knew the turf. Steele showed up in Black spaces. Churches, chambers, neighborhoods. And it *mattered*.

Larry Hogan followed suit. Boyd Rutherford picked up the baton—quiet, strategic, consistent.

Now we have Governor Wes Moore—and we're seeing the long game pay off.

Thanks to his leadership—and the persistence of State Senator Antonio Hayes—nearly $50 million has been committed to the West North Avenue Development Authority. A direct response to the

2015 Freddie Gray uprising, finally addressing decades of neglect.

The world saw boarded-up homes on TV and blamed the protests for the destruction. But we know the truth: those homes had been abandoned, neglected, and forgotten long before the cameras ever arrived.

Now, after years of inaction, change is finally happening.

Governor Ehrlich invested millions into Coppin. Hogan and Rutherford followed through. Moore is building on that foundation—with precision.

Because Senator Hayes *never* stopped pushing.

Now, Citywide Youth Empowerment, home to *Made in Bmore Clothing* and *Frozen Desert Sorbet*, operates from a $4 million building just blocks west of Penn-North. The Mill food court next to Coppin is open. That corridor hasn't felt this alive in decades.

For too long, Black communities offered loyalty and received only crumbs in return.
That is changing. By proving to the Maryland Democratic Party that Black voters have choices, we shifted the political landscape.

That single shift unlocked the kind of investment that has been long overdue.

Mindset.

That's what connects Mayor Marion Barry, Congressman Parren J. Mitchell, and every visionary Black leader who ever moved the needle—from Frederick Douglass to Reginald F. Lewis, from Clifton R. Wharton Jr. to today's Dave Steward and Roger Ferguson. They each saw what didn't yet exist, believed in it fully, and then brought it to life. It started in the mind.

They say if a cat wants to become a lion, it must lose its appetite for rats.

Too many of us remain trapped in old cycles—old habits, old thinking, old playbooks. Entire families, even whole cities, can grow addicted to the familiar, even when it's failing us. But a new generation is rising. Fast. They're digital. They're disruptive. They move differently. And our role is to root them in wisdom, even as they sprint ahead with innovation.

We must teach them: with privilege comes purpose. And that unity isn't performative. It's not for the group chat. It's not for social media. Real solidarity is quiet. Strategic. Sacred. It's for the long game.

Perhaps this time, we shouldn't rely on a singular leader—history has shown us the risks faced by charismatic Black leadership in America.

Instead, what we need is a collective mindset—one that spans from Bowie to Baltimore, from church pews to corporate boardrooms. A mindset united by shared priorities: rebuilding public education, generating lasting wealth, and moving in lockstep toward true, sustainable power.

The Maverick — Robert Lee "Bob" Clay

In my world of media, business, and politics in Baltimore, no one fought harder for Black-owned businesses than Robert Lee "Bob" Clay.

He was found shot to death on May 16, 2005. Officially, it was ruled a suicide. But the facts don't add up. Bob was right-handed. The bullet entered the left side of his head. That defies logic.

At the time, then-Mayor Martin O'Malley was campaigning for Governor. And Bob Clay? He was running just as hard *against* him—traveling the I-95 corridor from Laurel to Baltimore, from Prince George's County to Annapolis, warning voters not to support O'Malley.

That was Clay: fearless, focused, relentless.

He was a steadfast supporter of Delegate Jill Carter, even backing her mayoral campaign. As head of the Maryland Minority Contractors Association, Bob hosted monthly gatherings for Black business owners, especially in construction—a field he knew inside and out. But more than knowledge, he led by example.

Bob Clay wasn't about talk. He was action. He was accountability. He was that rare kind of man who didn't just demand results—he delivered them.

The last time I saw Bob, he came to Sandtown to pay me for work I'd done for him. Most folks get uneasy in these streets. Not Bob. He didn't flinch. He walked straight up to my door like a man raised on respect. That's something my father would have done.

Bob was a soldier. A warrior for Black empowerment. He stepped to anybody, anytime, anywhere. His death still hurts. His killer was never found. But those of us who knew him—who saw him fight for us—we carry the torch. His fight didn't end with him. It lives on in every corner of Baltimore's political and economic battleground.

Because the struggle for Black empowerment is far from over. It's woven into every campaign, every community effort, every election where the stakes are survival and self-determination.

Closing Reflection

Black business has always been more than commerce—it is a cornerstone of political power and community sovereignty. As this chapter shows, economic strength fuels political influence, and when Black businesses unite with clear purpose and strategy, they become a force that shapes policy, drives investment, and demands accountability.

Baltimore's history teaches us that Black entrepreneurship and political leadership have long walked hand in hand—from the faith leaders and professors of the Goon Squad to the modern-day champions revitalizing West North Avenue. Yet the path is never easy, and the stakes have never been higher. We must recognize that unity is not a feel-good concept or a hashtag; it is disciplined, structured, and relentless work—work that transcends egos and embraces a collective vision for lasting power.

The legacy of leaders like Robert Lee "Bob" Clay reminds us that the fight for Black economic and political empowerment is a marathon, not a sprint. His spirit lives on in those who continue to push against barriers, invest in our communities, and hold systems accountable.

Today, we stand at a crossroads. We have the blueprint and the examples—both from history and from the bold, new generation rising with digital savvy and fierce purpose. The choice is ours: Will we settle for crumbs, or will we claim the full measure of our power? Will we hold fast to old cycles, or will we embrace a collective mindset that spans neighborhoods, boardrooms, and ballots alike?

Black business is political power. And that power is the key to reshaping our future—one built on wealth, education, and true self-determination. The question is: Are we ready to own it?

CHAPTER 8

GREATER BALTIMORE POLITICS
SHEILA DIXON FOR MAYOR, 2016

When Sheila Dixon launched her comeback campaign in 2016, my PR firm had already worked with three Maryland governors. We knew the political terrain. We put in the work. So her loss wasn't just disappointing, it was painful. We believed her return was not only possible but necessary.

Now, I don't speak ill of the ancestors, but this needs to be said: **Armstead Jones**, in my view, played a pivotal role in her defeat.

Baltimore City had **over 1,800 voting irregularities**, compared to just 200 across the other 23 jurisdictions in the state. That's not a footnote—it's a crisis.

Formerly incarcerated voters—legally eligible—were turned away. Polling stations were plagued with confusion and misinformation. It didn't feel like an election. It felt like a setup.

And it wasn't just the election board. The media did its part. Outlets like Fox News made sure Dixon's past mistakes drowned out her present vision. We've seen this strategy before: destroy the Black leader—not just physically, but through character assassination.

Was Dixon perfect? No. But she was effective, bold, and a staunch advocate for Black-owned businesses. That made her a threat.

There is a white power structure in Baltimore that operates with quiet precision. Black politicians are often given two choices: comply or be crushed. But as Congressman Parren Mitchell reminded us, our vote must be **ours**—not for sale, not for lease.

The powers that be feared Sheila Dixon would return **on her terms**. And they were right.

Still, we made history: our team pushed for a recount, and the Baltimore Board of Elections **decertified the vote**—a rare, unprecedented move. It was a statement. A warning. And a reminder that the people are watching.

Randallstown: A Community I Love

Let me be clear: I love Randallstown. I've been going there since I was a teen to visit family. I remember Cook's on Liberty and Rolling Road. Sista's Place was always the spot. I've played ball at Scotts Branch. I even served as founding editor of *Northwest Voice* under Kenny Brown.

I've seen this community's greatness.

I remember Ken Oliver—our first Black County Councilman. He helped bring a Walmart, Home Depot, a sit-down restaurant, the Liberty Road athletic center, and a resource hub to the corridor. His fish fries were legendary. His political impact—deep and often under-credited.

I remember the late Ella White Campbell, who sat Aaron Barnett and me at her table and had a heart-to-heart about unity. She was "Big Mama"—a boss, a truth-teller, and an unapologetic Black matriarch who didn't play games when it came to community.

And Dr. Cheryl Pasteur—an icon of education. She taught not just children but adults. And now she carries that same fire to Annapolis. These are the kinds of leaders we need more of—unafraid, unapologetic, and deeply rooted in love for our people.

This is the assignment. This is the moment.

We must honor the past while seizing the future. With strategy. With unity. And above all, with mindset.

Real Black political power in Maryland has never come from parties or platforms—it comes from organized economic strength, disciplined alliances, and a deep understanding of how the game is played.

And in this game, the most valuable commodity is trust.

Edwin Johnson embodied that kind of trust. His loyalty helped Carl Stokes move mountains. When Verna Jones served as State Senator for the 44th, a brother named Anis stood firmly by her side. Larry Young had Bill Wiley as his confidant. These weren't just supporters—they were the backbone. In politics, trust and loyalty are everything.

That's why Martin O'Malley likely called his brother Peter first. And why countless candidates have called Julius Henson over the years. Every serious political player has a core team—a tight circle that they can depend on without question. If you have one person like that, you're blessed. Two? That's a Godsend.

Because politics is public, discretion is power. You need people around you who can not only be trusted, but who can also deliver—every time. From campaign treasurers to social media managers, from signage crews to speechwriters, from volunteer coordinators to media strategists—every role matters. The best campaigns are structured like high-functioning businesses. Everything must be intentional. Every dollar. Every step. Every message.

The sharpest candidates understand this and invest accordingly. The pros hire pros. The rookies overspend or trust the wrong people—and it shows. For example, a seasoned veteran like Sheila Dixon can do more with less than most can with double the resources. Why? Because she knows the terrain and how to deploy her team strategically.

Running for office isn't a walk in the park—it's a political decathlon. A candidate has to manage addresses and emails, build press relationships, energize volunteers, oversee the money, and more—all at once. You need a team. And not just any team—a trusted, competent one. This is the business of politics. Run it like one.

Even the details matter. Attire, for instance, may seem minor, but optics count. For men: blue or gray suit, white shirt, red or blue tie. For women: professional, business-ready attire. It's not about conformity—it's about signaling that you understand the basics. Once you master them, you can innovate from there.

So no—it's not about party loyalty or campaign platforms. It's about infrastructure. Discipline. Strategy. Trust. That's how real Black political power is built and sustained. Not by hoping for inclusion, but by mastering the game and owning your position on the board.

The First Black Governor of Maryland

In the early stages of Maryland's gubernatorial race, Wes Moore was polling in the single digits. At the time, Comptroller Peter Franchot was the presumed frontrunner. He had been eyeing the Governor's Mansion since the O'Malley years and carried himself like it was already his.

But Franchot made a critical miscalculation: He ignored the broader Black community.

He leaned on symbolic gestures—passing out gold tokens engraved with his name at public events—as if trinkets and photo ops were enough to earn Black votes. It was tone-deaf and superficial. Just like Kathleen Kennedy-Townsend before him, Franchot moved from a place of entitlement. He assumed support from Black voters would come automatically.

One moment told us everything. At a gubernatorial forum focused on Minority Business Enterprise (MBE)—in a room full of Black entrepreneurs and community leaders—Franchot took the mic, said his wife was sick, and left. His parting message? "Check my website to see what I have planned for MBE."

It was tasteless. Disrespectful. And it showed exactly how little he valued the voices, votes, and economic future of Black Marylanders.

He underestimated us—and paid the price.

Wes Moore's rise from underdog to Maryland's first Black governor wasn't just a political win—it was a declaration. A declaration that when we organize, unify, and show up on our terms, Black political power isn't just possible; it's unstoppable.

But winning elections is only one part of the battle. True power—lasting power—comes when we control our story, build economic strength, and shape the systems around us. That's the foundation of our Blueprint.

So, with this victory as a turning point, we turn the page to the next chapter of our movement—a chapter about owning our narrative, wielding political influence, and expanding our reach from Baltimore to the world.

Closing Reflection: Politics as Power, Strategy, and Stewardship

Politics is not just about winning elections—it's about building the infrastructure, trust, and discipline that turn victories into lasting power. From the setbacks of Sheila Dixon's campaign to the historic breakthrough of Wes Moore, we see that Black political power demands more than passion; it requires strategy, unity, and an unwavering commitment to community.

We must remember that political battles are also cultural ones—fought with narratives, optics, and alliances as much as votes. The systems designed to hold us back are real, and so is the quiet work of organizing, building trusted teams, and mastering every detail. But those who understand the game—and play it with integrity and resilience—hold the keys to change.

Baltimore and Maryland's story is a microcosm of the broader movement. It teaches us that real power is rooted in economics, relationships, and disciplined execution. Our elected leaders are important, but they must be supported by a community that owns its voice and its vision.

As we look forward, the challenge is clear: not just to elect Black leaders, but to ensure they lead with the resources, strategy, and accountability that transform promises into progress. This chapter closes, but the movement continues—stronger, wiser, and ready to claim its rightful place on the political stage.

The future of Greater Baltimore politics is ours to shape. Let's build it with purpose.

CHAPTER 9

WE DO HAVE POWER

In earlier chapters, we laid the foundation for Black economic empowerment. Now, we turn to another essential pillar of our Blueprint for Black Power: reclaiming our narrative and political influence. Controlling the story we tell—and choosing leaders who truly represent us—fuels every strategy outlined in this book.

1. Mastering the Media Narrative

I've heard the refrain—"this is a white man's world"—so often it's become background noise. But expertise transcends race, and true value lies in skills and vision. I chase that truth through media. For too long, mainstream outlets—from D.W. Griffith's *The Birth of a Nation* to today's crime-heavy newscasts—have framed Black life through fear and stereotypes. While newswire stories may be neutral, editors choose which frames dominate, making crime—not achievement—the default narrative.

Blueprint Action: Launch or support Black-owned media platforms. Publish at least one positive deep-dive story about Black innovators, families, or communities each week. Shift perceptions by amplifying success stories.

2. Symbolic Victories, Strategic Momentum

Barack Obama's presidency showed how image and reality intertwine. The Obama family—father, mother, two daughters—offered a powerful counter-narrative to the 70% single-mother statistic in Black America. This wasn't just symbolism; it inspired millions to see new possibilities. Likewise, a photo of Governor Wes Moore, Congressman Kweisi Mfume, President David Wilson (Morgan State), and Mayor Brandon Scott standing together at a Baltimore science center speaks volumes: four Black leaders, united, rewriting our city's future.

Blueprint Action: Identify and promote four local Black leaders in politics, education, business, and media. Organize a community event recognizing their achievements and networking needs.

3. Voting Power and Political Strategy

We are nearly 14% of the U.S. population—and also roughly 14% of the global population, over a billion strong worldwide. Yet, our political engagement and turnout rates often lag. Voting is more than a right—it's leverage. From local school boards to city councils and state legislatures, these elected bodies hold the levers of change. Every ballot cast increases our power to negotiate policies, budgets, and laws.

Blueprint Action: Launch a "14 & Counting" voter registration and turnout campaign. Aim for a 75% turnout among eligible Black voters in your district's next election.

4. Global Context: From Berlin to AfCFTA

The 1884–85 Berlin Conference carved Africa into European colonies—without a single African voice at the table. Those arbitrary borders still shape today's neocolonial trade patterns and debt burdens. But alternatives exist: Botswana's resource sovereignty, Burkina Faso's grassroots economic programs, and the African Continental Free Trade Area (AfCFTA). By lowering tariffs and harmonizing regulations, AfCFTA could boost intra-African trade by 50%, lift 30 million people out of poverty, and keep wealth on the continent.

Blueprint Action: Establish a Pan-African Business Circle in your city. Facilitate at least one import–

export partnership between a local Black-owned business and an African counterpart each quarter.

5. Financial Independence and Reparative Justice

True sovereignty requires financial autonomy. Heavy debt and conditional lending trap many African nations—and Black entrepreneurs—in cycles of dependency. We must demand debt relief, create sovereign wealth funds, and expand local-currency settlements. Reparations—land, cultural, and policy reforms—must accompany these economic strategies, ensuring that addressing past injustices underpins our future prosperity.

Blueprint Action: Partner with a financial think tank to draft a white paper on African-American–African reparations frameworks. Present findings at a community town hall within six months.

6. Cultural and Intellectual Decolonization

Decolonizing our minds accelerates all other goals. Moving beyond romanticized "pre-colonial" myths, we embrace a culture of resistance and innovation. From combat literature to jazz, hip hop, and Afrofuturism, our art and scholarship reflect lived realities and chart new futures.

Blueprint Action: Curate a quarterly speaker series featuring Pan-African artists, writers, and scholars discussing decolonization in practice.

Conclusion: Our Moment, Our Movement

Yes—we have power. More than many realize. But power demands action: controlling our narrative, winning elections, forging global partnerships, securing financial independence, and reshaping culture. This Blueprint ties every point together, showing how to build influence at every level. Turn these pages into movement, and let's claim our power—together.

From Vision to Execution: The Blueprint in Action

To truly activate this blueprint, we need partnerships that turn ideas into infrastructure. One organization that exemplifies this principle—working at the intersection of policy, capital, and community—is the U.S. Black Chambers, Inc. Under the visionary leadership of Ron Busby, Sr., they are not just building businesses—they are helping to architect the future of Black economic power.

Closing Reflection: Claiming Our Power, Shaping Our Future

We stand at a pivotal moment in history—a time when the threads of narrative, political influence, economic sovereignty, and cultural identity intertwine to create unprecedented possibilities for Black empowerment. The power we hold is real, but it is not automatic. It must be claimed, wielded, and expanded through intentional action and collective commitment.

Our stories, our leaders, and our votes are the foundation of this power. By reshaping the narrative, we redefine who we are and what we can achieve. By stepping into the political arena with purpose, we secure the policies that protect and uplift our communities. By forging global connections and demanding reparative justice, we open new pathways to wealth and sovereignty. And by decolonizing our culture and intellect, we ignite creativity and resilience that will fuel generations to come.

This is not just a blueprint on paper—it is a call to movement, a summons to partnership, and a charge to every individual ready to build a future where Black power is undeniable, unshakable, and enduring.

Our moment is now. The power is ours. Let us rise, together.

CHAPTER 10

PARTNERING FOR POWER—THE U.S. BLACK CHAMBERS

In our *Black Blueprint,* partnerships amplify impact. Few relationships embody this truth better than the one between *BMORENews* and the U.S. Black Chambers under the visionary leadership of Ron Busby, Sr. As President and CEO, Ron has transformed the U.S. Black Chambers into a strategic engine for policy, capital, and capacity building—making it a cornerstone of our collective trajectory.

Why the U.S. Black Chambers Matters Ron Busby's unwavering support of BMORENews.com—appearing on our programs to spotlight entrepreneurs, share policy insights, and strengthen our multimedia platforms—mirrors the sophistication and rigor he brings to every initiative. Under his stewardship, the U.S. Black Chambers has elevated Black business ownership from grassroots hustle to national policy priority.

Six Pillars of Collective Empowerment: These six strategic axes form the foundation upon which Ron and his team build Black business power:

1. Advocacy
   Fighting for bipartisan legislation that dismantles barriers—from discrimination in lending to inequitable contracting. By engaging lawmakers across the spectrum, the U.S. Black Chambers ensures Black entrepreneurs have a seat at every policy table.
2. Access to Capital
   Partnering with community banks, credit unions, and institutional investors to unlock loans, lines of credit, and equity investments. More capital means more startups, expansions, and jobs.
3. Contracting Opportunities
   Leveling the playing field in public and private procurement through bid-readiness workshops, certification assistance, and capacity-building resources. When Black firms win contracts, entire communities prosper.
4. Entrepreneurial Training
   Delivering rigorous programming in

financial management, marketing strategy, and leadership development. Equipped with these skills, Black business owners outcompete and outlast.

5. Chamber Development
   Strengthening local Black chambers through technical assistance, peer networking, and leadership coaching—and seeding new chapters in underserved areas. A national network of chambers multiplies our influence and resources.
6. Information & Technology
   Advocating for digital equity, providing market intelligence, and leveraging media partnerships to ensure Black-owned businesses stay ahead of emerging trends and technologies.

2025–2026 BLACKprint: Their Next Frontier
Building on these pillars, the U.S. Black Chambers' annual policy roadmap—the BLACKprint—focuses on five critical priorities:

1. Market Access: Expanding government, global, and e-commerce channels for Black enterprises.

2. Proven Development Programs: Scaling initiatives that deliver demonstrable growth and resilience.
3. Next-Gen Entrepreneurs: Mentorship, seed funding, and curricula to empower young Black innovators.
4. Wealth-Building Policies: Tax reforms, M&A pathways, and contract equity that foster generational wealth.
5. Digital Inclusion: Investment and advocacy to close the technology gap for Black entrepreneurs.

Call to Action: Be a Partner in Power Our movement demands more than awareness—it requires active participation. Here's how you can plug into this powerhouse partnership:

1. Join the U.S. Black Chambers. Become a member or renew your membership to access resources, networks, and policy influence.

2. Amplify the Voice. Feature U.S. Black Chambers leaders and programs on your media channels—podcasts, newsletters, and social feeds.

3. Invest Locally. Partner with Black-owned financial institutions to fund fellow entrepreneurs in your community.

4. Champion Policy. Contact your elected officials to support BLACKprint priorities—share the roadmap, testify at hearings, and track legislation.

5. Cultivate the Next Generation. Mentor a young Black entrepreneur, or sponsor entrepreneur training programs through your organization.

By leveraging the U.S. Black Chambers' infrastructure and expertise alongside BMORENews' storytelling power, we forge a partnership that turns strategy into action. Let's stand with Ron Busby and the U.S. Black Chambers—because our Blueprint for Black Power is only as strong as the alliances we build.

The Oakland Connection—Cathy Adams and Local Power

In our journey to build Black power from the ground up, we often look to national organizations—and rightfully so. Yet, the true engines of community resilience are local leaders who know their streets, storefronts, and struggles intimately. One such leader is Cathy Adams, President of the Oakland African American Chamber of Commerce (OAACC). Busby introduced us. Cathy's story illustrates why grassroots chambers matter—and how one visionary can transform crisis into opportunity.

Herculean Leadership Under Pressure Running a Black chamber of commerce is no small task; it demands 24/7 commitment with no days off. Cathy Adams exemplifies this tenacity. Early in her tenure, she faced the same uphill climb that many chamber presidents know well: scarce resources, relentless advocacy, and a community's high expectations. Then, COVID-19 struck. Businesses shuttered overnight, and entire livelihoods hung in the balance.

Most chambers scrambled; some paused. Cathy sprang into action. Recognizing that stabilization required swift capital infusion, she launched a microgrant program, personally securing funding, and distributing $63,000 in $1,000 grants to 63 member businesses at the height of the pandemic. These grants weren't just checks—they were lifelines that kept doors open and spirits high.

Why Oakland Matters Founded in 2003, the OAACC has advanced economic opportunity for Black entrepreneurs across Oakland. Under Cathy's leadership, the chamber has:

1. **Expanded Access** to business advising, minority certification assistance, and notary services.
2. **Curated Workshops** on financial management, marketing, and digital tools.
3. **Amplified Voices** at city hall, advocating for equitable contracting and municipal support.

By celebrating Black heritage through cultural events and building solidarity among members, OAACC doesn't just grow businesses—it strengthens community bonds.

Blueprint Action: Cultivate Your Local Chamber

1. **Identify Your Chamber Leader:** Research the president or executive director of your local Black chamber. Reach out and schedule a listening session to understand their top three challenges.

2. **Support a Microgrant Initiative:** Partner with local funders—city councilmembers, tech firms, philanthropic foundations—to seed a $10,000 microgrant pool for 10 Black-owned businesses.

3. **Amplify Locally:** Dedicate a regular media spotlight—podcast, newsletter article, or social post—to highlight one chamber member's success story each month.

4. **Volunteer Expertise:** Offer pro bono services—legal counsel, marketing strategy, bookkeeping—to an OAACC member or similar chamber associates.

Call to Action

Cathy Adams didn't wait for someone else to lead during crisis—she rose to the moment. That's what real grown people do: they see a problem and they fix it. Now, it's our turn. Whether you're a community organizer, corporate sponsor, or fellow entrepreneur, you can partner with chambers like OAACC to multiply impact. Seek out your local Black chamber, invest time or capital, and help unleash the power of grassroots leadership. Together, we build a network of Oakland connections across every city—because true Black power begins in our neighborhoods.

But neighborhood power is just the beginning.

To truly embody Black excellence and liberation, we must go deeper—beyond programs and policies, into the spirit and mindset that fueled movements like Tulsa's Greenwood. In other words, we must reclaim Black Wall Street not just as history, but as a way of life.

CHAPTER 11

BLACK WALL STREET AS A MINDSET: LESSONS FROM DR. MICHAEL CARTER

When I met Dr. Michael Carter Sr. in 2011—the national president of Black Wall Street USA—my understanding of Black Wall Street was transformed. I had long admired Tulsa's Greenwood District as a historic symbol of Black excellence and economic self-sufficiency. But Dr. Carter shifted my focus: Black Wall Street is not just a place—it's a mindset. A Kingdom-driven mission. A spiritual and economic calling.

His words echoed deeply within me, becoming the very title of my book: *I Am Black Wall Street*. And his lesson was clear:
"If God ain't in it, it ain't Black Wall Street."

In this chapter, I share Dr. Carter's spiritual-economic blueprint—a framework rooted in faith, humility, and community restoration. It's a call to build with purpose and power.

1. The Right Spirit: Laying the Foundation

1. Surrendering Ego: True leadership begins with humility. We must trade ambition for alignment—allowing divine purpose to guide our steps.

2. Hearing God's Voice: Success is spiritual before it is material. Through prayer, fasting, and discernment, we gain clarity on the right moves at the right time.

3. Daily Humility Checks: Pride, fear, and doubt are distractions. Consistent prayer and accountability keep us grounded and responsive to the Spirit.

2. Spiritual Mapping: Finding Your Black Wall Street

1. Follow God's Lead: Just as the Israelites were led to promised land, we must ask: *Where is God sending us?* Seek divine guidance for the neighborhoods, blocks, or corridors in need of revival.

2. Prayer Walks: Walk the land. Intercede for the people. Declare God's presence. Identify spiritual strongholds and community needs.

3. Claim the Ground: Speak life over each storefront, home, and vacant lot. Proclaim them as territory for God's Kingdom — economically, culturally, and spiritually.

3. Spiritual Leadership: Qualities for Kingdom Builders

1. Servant Leadership: Lead as Christ led — with sacrifice, grace, and purpose. Uplift others. Build ecosystems that support entrepreneurs, families, and institutions.

2. Accountability Circles: Create peer and mentor groups that promote transparency, correction, and spiritual growth. Nobody builds alone.

3. Visionary Faith: Hold the vision when no one else can see it. Speak hope when the numbers say "no." Faith is the engine.

4. Kingdom Building: Community Restoration in Action

1. Economic Stewardship: Launch initiatives like the *Black Wealth Initiative*—including real estate investment, cooperative economics, and financial literacy to build generational wealth.

2. Healing the Wounds: Address trauma. Offer emotional and spiritual support. Restore not just buildings but people.

3. Educating the Next Generation: Build programs that merge practical business skills with Kingdom values. Train builders, not just workers.

5. Honoring the Ancestors, Fueling the Future

From O.W. Gurley and B.C. Franklin to Dr. A.C. Jackson and Ada Huff, the pioneers of Black Wall Street showed us what faith-rooted enterprise looks like. We honor them not just by remembering, but by *building*.

As Scripture reminds us:

"Not by might, nor by power, but by My Spirit," says the Lord. – *Zechariah 4:6*

Call to Action: Activating the Mindset

1. Pray & Plan – Assemble a core team and fast together for 24 hours. Ask God to reveal your target neighborhood and community needs.

2. Host a Spiritual Mapping Session – Invite pastors, business owners, and residents to map out your city's assets, challenges, and spiritual gateways.

3. Launch a Kingdom Business Incubator – Partner with local churches or organizations to run a 12-week program blending business training with spiritual formation.

4. Commission Quarterly Prayer Walks – Mobilize intercessors to walk your designated corridor and speak God's favor over the land.

5. Tell the Story – Use your media platform to spotlight your local "Black Wall Street" in motion. Testify. Inspire others to rise.

Living Example:

Jacqueline "Jacqui" Cummings — Baltimore's Black Wall Street on 25th Street

One of the first people I connected Dr. Carter with was a Baltimore powerhouse: Jacqueline Cummings. A true SheEO, Jacqui owns five buildings on West 25th Street and has created space for 31 Black-owned businesses within just two city blocks.

That stretch of 25th Street has become one of the most vibrant concentrations of Black entrepreneurship in the city — a modern-day Black Wall Street in action.

Her work is bold, intentional, and Spirit-led. It's proof that when we combine faith, strategy, and community love, we build not just businesses — we build legacies.

Through her nonprofit, **Notre Maison Connects**, Cummings has led a revival of community-focused economic development. She spearheaded initiatives like the **Black Wall Street Expos**, youth-focused programs such as the **Greater Youth Initiative**, and wellness efforts including **blood drives** and **literacy campaigns**. In 2023, she successfully worked with **Mayor Brandon Scott** to officially designate the corridor as **"Black Wall Street on 25th Street,"** drawing inspiration from Tulsa's historic Greenwood District.

Cummings has also launched **The Chill Spot @ Notre Maison**, a café and community hub that offers refreshments, social space, and youth employment. Her work continues to draw new businesses—ranging from clothing shops to tech labs—while strengthening pride, unity, and economic power within Baltimore's Black community.

Jacqui Cummings is not just preserving legacy—she's building the future of Black Wall Street in Baltimore. Her work reminds us what's possible when vision meets action. But for every corridor being reclaimed, there's a fight to keep legacy from being erased. Her work reminds us what's possible when vision meets action—but for every corridor reclaimed, there's another where legacy is under threat.

One of those defenders is Quianna Cooke—a Baltimore City educator, activist, and former political candidate—who lives in the historic neighborhood of Hoe's Heights.

Hoe's Heights: Legacy, Land, and the Line We Keep Crossing

I've known Quianna Cooke for years—a passionate, principled educator in Baltimore City Public Schools, a fierce advocate, and former political candidate. She's not the kind of person who watches injustice unfold in silence. So when she called me about a barrier cutting off her community from Roland Avenue, I could hear the urgency in her voice.

Quianna lives near West Lafayette and Wheeler Avenues—an area I know well. I played James Mosher Baseball just up the block at School #144. Down the hill past Winchester Apartments was Calverton Heights—a neighborhood where people took care of their lawns, knew their neighbors, and held onto values that built legacy.

I have deep roots in this part of Baltimore. My 95-year-old Aunt Edythe still lives nearby. My maternal grandmother lived in the 2300 blocks of Harlem Avenue. Our family church, Perkins Square Baptist, stands in the 2500 block of Edmondson Avenue. My first girlfriend lived just around the corner. I had friends from the neighborhood and baseball teammates scattered throughout. I proudly delivered Afro-American Newspapers throughout this thoughtful, connected community.

Quianna is no stranger to standing up against injustice. Kind yet resolute, when something doesn't sit right, she acts. So when she called me about her historic neighborhood of Hoe's Heights in North Baltimore, I knew something serious was happening.

She told me the community was being cut off—literally. A physical barrier had been erected to block Hoe's Heights residents from accessing Roland Avenue, their direct link to surrounding neighborhoods. When I arrived, she introduced me to a chapter of Baltimore history I hadn't fully known—and it made my blood boil.

Hoe's Heights was founded by Grandison Hoe, a free Black man. His descendants still live there. Though the neighborhood is now multiracial, its Black legacy remains foundational. What Roland Park residents had done—cutting off a historic Black community—felt painfully familiar. It wasn't just inconsiderate. It was history repeating itself.

Baltimore is no stranger to racially motivated urban design, and we had to respond.

In 1910, Baltimore Mayor J. Barry Mahool signed into law the nation's first racial zoning ordinance, forbidding Black residents from moving onto white-majority blocks and vice versa. Though later overturned, this legislation laid the groundwork for modern redlining—a term and practice that originated right here in Baltimore. The city became a national blueprint for systematically disinvesting in Black communities through housing policy.

And yet, despite all this, Baltimore's Black communities have built beautiful, resilient neighborhoods.

Wilson Park and Morgan Park are two such places. Located in Northeast Baltimore, these early Black suburbs were built by and for African Americans in the early 20th century. Homeownership was more than property—it was power. These neighborhoods were intentionally developed to give Black families refuge from the indignities of segregation and economic exclusion. Generations of Black professionals, educators, clergy, and civic leaders built lives there—quietly resisting systems stacked against them.

Hoe's Heights is part of that same legacy. Just like Brooklyn's Weeksville—a free Black community founded in the 1830s by James Weeks—or Seneca Village in Manhattan, which was erased to make room for Central Park, these Black enclaves were about more than shelter. They represented self-determination, ownership, and freedom.

That's why I chose to host a Black Wall Street Awards ceremony at the Weeksville Heritage Center in Brooklyn. It was a full-circle moment: honoring today's Black entrepreneurs and leaders in a space born of our ancestors' courage. It tied our present to our past in a way that words alone cannot. These awards help preserve legacy and shed light where people have tried to bury the truth.

In Hoe's Heights, we helped bring that truth forward. We used our platforms to elevate the issue. Eventually, the barrier was removed. But the real victory was in the awareness it sparked.

This wasn't just about road access. It was about the audacity to exist and thrive in a system that was never built for us.

Today, more people know about Hoe's Heights. More understand how Baltimore—home to both racial segregation ordinances and Black excellence—embodies the tension and promise of America.

Our neighborhoods matter. Our stories matter. And every time we lift them up—whether through journalism, community organizing, or honoring our own—we take one more step toward justice.

Closing Reflection: Embracing the Black Wall Street Mindset

Black Wall Street is far more than a historic place—it's a living mindset rooted in faith, resilience, and collective purpose. Dr. Michael Carter's powerful reminder, "If God ain't in it, it ain't Black Wall Street," calls us to lead with humility, spiritual clarity, and unwavering commitment to community restoration.

The examples of Jacqueline Cummings and Quianna Cooke show us what happens when vision meets action, when faith blends with strategy, and when legacy is both honored and fiercely defended. From Baltimore's 25th Street corridor to Hoe's Heights, Black Wall Street lives on in the courage to reclaim space, the determination to build wealth, and the resolve to protect our neighborhoods from erasure.

Our task is clear: to adopt this Kingdom-driven mindset, to map our communities with purpose, and to build ecosystems where economic empowerment and spiritual growth thrive side by side. This work demands more than ambition—it requires a spirit-led commitment to uplift every generation that follows.

As we face systemic challenges and continue the fight for equity, let us remember the ancestors who paved the way and the present-day builders who keep the flame alive. The Black Wall Street mindset calls us not just to dream, but to do—rooted in faith, fueled by unity, and dedicated to justice.

The journey continues. Let us rise with purpose, knowing that our work is sacred, our legacy enduring, and our future bright.

CHAPTER 12

BLACK WALL STREET NATION: FROM HARLEM TO THE HEART OF THE SOUTH

"We've always built. We've always resisted. And I've been on the ground, witnessing and defending our legacy—with a pen, a mic, a camera, and a platform."

New York has always held a certain kind of magic. For me, it became more than just a destination—it became a proving ground, a media capital where the Black Wall Street movement could stretch its legs and plant new roots.

I first met Jet Miller, one of the most accomplished makeup artists I know, during this journey. An Aries by birth and a boss by nature, Jet is pure fire. Her story resonated deeply because it mirrored a truth I've always felt in my gut: Baltimore breeds hustlers. Real ones. The kind who turn grit into gold. We're not DC. We're not Philly. And we're definitely not New York. This is Baltimore. We've got our own flavor—Old Bay and ambition.

I've seen that spirit in others, like Xavier Sharif of Xavier Furs, who built a national luxury brand; Mario Armstrong, a household name in tech; and Dr. David Miller, a close brother who took fatherhood advocacy global. Baltimore builds differently: we create because we must, innovate because we've had to. Akio Evans transforms Nike Air Force Ones into wearable art for celebrities—and commands top dollar doing it. And of course, there's Reginald F. Lewis, the legend who executed the largest-ever overseas takeover of a U.S. company at the time—from Baltimore. We come from that cloth.

That's the tradition I've always longed to be part of. It's the fire I saw in Jet, who told me she traveled to New York three or four times a month just to sharpen her craft. "I wanted to be among the best," she said. And New York was where they were. That stayed with me. I realized I had to do the same. If I was serious about building a media brand with reach and relevance, I needed to show up where the stakes were highest—and the lights were brightest.

I took that dream and shared it with Peggy Morris of *Sisters4Sisters Network, Inc.* I told her I wanted to bring the newly launched awards to New York

City. The late Bob Ingram, a trusted ally, connected me with someone at the United Nations. And just like that, my kids and I were headed to New York for the *BMORENews* Global Forum on Women's Empowerment. Back then, the Joe Manns Black Wall Street Awards were still called the Black Capital Awards.

That was 2012. Since then, we've hosted the awards in Brooklyn twice—once at the Weeksville Heritage Center, and again at Brooklyn Borough Hall, thanks to then-Borough President Eric Adams. Adams had long supported our Black economic efforts in Harlem, through the leadership of Walter Edwards, the Godfather of Harlem. Walter predicted Adams' rise before most even considered it. He believed in him early. Today, Eric Adams is the Mayor of New York City.

Our work in New York has evolved into something greater than I imagined. The awards became a platform not just to celebrate Black entrepreneurship—but also to uplift advocates for justice. Thanks to connections from Peggy and my dear friend Odessa Hopkins, we were introduced to Victor Pate, a towering figure in the movement to end solitary confinement and uplift formerly incarcerated individuals.

Pate's work is critical. The U.S. has just 5% of the world's population but 25% of its incarcerated people. Black men make up nearly 40% of those imprisoned, and Black women are the fastest-growing demographic behind bars. That's not a statistic—that's a system. A crisis. A business model designed to disappear us.

In Harlem, we made it a point to recognize those reversing mass incarceration alongside entrepreneurs. From Walter Edwards to Victor Pate, these men are generals in the Big Apple's frontline struggle for justice.

And through it all, New York has always shown love. I'd be remiss if I didn't mention my brother Lee Vaughan, who's driven me to and from NYC so many times I've lost count. He laughs because I act like a kid on Christmas every time we cross the George Washington Bridge. And he's right. I do.

Because every time I enter that city, it reminds me: We belong here. Our people belong in rooms of power, on stages of influence, and in stories of triumph. And I'm going to keep telling those stories—whether in Brooklyn, Harlem, Baltimore, or beyond.

The Harlem Business Alliance

Two remarkable business leaders from Baltimore connected me to the Godfather of Harlem—one of them even brought him right to my doorstep. When I stepped outside to meet him, I had no idea just how legendary this man truly is. His legacy speaks volumes: a builder of institutions, people, communities, and yes, even nations. Despite his monumental achievements, he remains a humble man, grounded by faith and humility. He's witty, yet wise—a source of confidence on days when doubt creeps in. Simply put, he's a confidence builder.

His Rolodex is vast, his connections monumental. Walk with him down 125th Street, and you'd think you were alongside a former president. But this is just Mr. Walter Edwards. He's a scholar, a devoted family man, and a creator of thriving businesses and empowered entrepreneurs.

Through Walter, I met Regina Smith—whom I regard as the Queen of Harlem. She once led the Harlem Business Alliance, and though I know many leaders, Regina exemplifies the visionary business leadership our communities desperately need. Over the years, we've hosted several Joe Manns Black Wall Street Awards at the Alliance's home on Malcolm X Boulevard. Our collaboration deepened when we worked together on the Black Economic Commission, a national effort that forged lasting bonds.

Just as our momentum was building, COVID struck. Yet, from that challenge emerged BlackUSA.News. Alongside Tasemere Gathers, we forged a streaming news network with hosts spanning New York, Baltimore, Washington D.C., Raleigh, Atlanta, Miami, Los Angeles, and Oakland. Among them, Doug Blacksher in Oakland stands out as a powerhouse. His passion for Black-owned businesses and political empowerment mirrors my own, and I'm deeply grateful for his contributions. Doug's relentless spirit—and the dedication of his team, including Kim—rejuvenates my resolve.

Doug's presence is a constant reminder that Tasemere and I are not alone. Across the country, a dedicated army fuels this Black-owned media company, proving that together, we're building something powerful and enduring.

Black Wall Street DURHAM

My dear friend Marsha Jews, my "ride or die" and relentless advocate for Black businesses and artists, introduced me to Dr. Eric Kelly one day. Marsha always brings solid intel and inspires action—that's just who she is.

When I connected with Doc, I quickly realized we share a deep passion for Black business empowerment. He runs the Black Business Olympics out of Charlotte—an international platform uniting speakers and entrepreneurs from across the African Diaspora. His tenacity and ability to bring people together are unmatched.

He's a man after my own heart. Whenever he calls, I answer. And he does the same. We often fill in for each other at the last minute, keeping the momentum going. What's more, Durham—along with Tulsa and Richmond—is officially recognized as one of the nation's three Black Wall Streets.

The mission behind the expo is powerful: to raise scholarships for students pursuing college education. We host a weeklong pitch event where students present their ideas and demonstrate their commitment to learning. We aim to award ten laptops and scholarships up to $10,000, depending on donations.

The theme for BLACK BUSINESS EXPO USA 2025 is "Economic Inclusion!" It's about that fire inside—the drive to speak up, make an impact, and harness your creativity to transform economic opportunities. This virtual week brings together creative leaders for sessions and workshops focused on challenging the status quo, securing financing, building and sustaining businesses, fostering corporate relationships, and reshaping the business world for the better.

Why does he present the expo? Because it's vital. He and his team do it for the students and entrepreneurs who reach out every day, seeking guidance and scholarships. The business gap and economic challenges are real, and without change, they will persist. We support students interested in business administration, science, technology, advertising, marketing, public policy, and entrepreneurship—encouraging them to start building businesses while still in school.

North Carolina is the 28th largest state in the country and ranks 8th in the Black American population. The Triangle—Raleigh, Durham, and Chapel Hill—has over 2.1 million residents. Imagine knowing just 500 of those people. With over $45 billion circulating in North Carolina's economy, the potential for Black business growth and economic empowerment here is enormous.

Black Wall Street: Atlanta

Returning to Atlanta with the Joe Manns Black Wall Street Awards is more than a homecoming—it's a full-circle moment.

Having attended Morehouse from '83 to '85, Atlanta will always hold a special place in my heart. It's where my roots as a leader began to take shape. It's where iron sharpened iron—and where excellence wasn't the exception, but the expectation. So when I bring Black Wall Street to the A, it's not just another stop. It's sacred ground.

I think of the incredible people who now call Atlanta home—Michelle Blue, Robert Scott, Bou Khan, my cousin Carlos, and my national president, Lee Vaughan. And I think of native Atlantans like my college landlord who served on City Council, Cleta Winslow, and my Veterans expert, Morocco Coleman. While I'm dropping names, let me lift up the giants whose shoulders we all stand on: Mayor Maynard Jackson and the legendary Herman J. Russell.

Their story isn't just Atlanta's story—it's a masterclass in Black empowerment.

You can't talk about Marion Barry without also invoking Maynard Jackson. He reshaped Atlanta's political and economic landscape with boldness and brilliance. From what I understand, Jackson laid down the law to prime contractors: if you want to do business with the city, you're going to hire Black Atlantans and subcontract to Black-owned companies. Period.

He didn't ask. He insisted. And in doing so, he opened the floodgates for a generation of Black wealth and enterprise. That kind of political courage created the Atlanta we know today—a city so rich in opportunity that many come for college and never look back. I've seen it time and again in the lives of people I know.

So, to not bring the Joe Manns Black Wall Street Awards to Atlanta? That's simply not an option.

We've honored excellence at iconic venues like Pascal's and the Absalom Jones Center. We've celebrated on historic Auburn Avenue and along the pulse of Peachtree. Every time, it feels electric—because Atlanta breathes Black entrepreneurship. You can feel it in the air. You can taste it in the hustle. And what makes it even more powerful is the presence of our brothers and sisters from across the African Diaspora—especially the Caribbean—all building, thriving, and contributing to a shared legacy of success.

This is my favorite kind of environment: where Black people are doing well in business. Where we're empowered, connected, and unapologetically building wealth. That's what I live for. That's why I do this work.

Atlanta doesn't just reflect what's possible—it is the possibility. And it's in cities like Atlanta, and organizations like Black Wall Street, where the seeds of true empowerment take root and grow strong.

This spirit of building and uplifting carries forward into every corner of our community. It's alive in the networks that nurture, the leaders who guide, and the brothers who stand together.

Which brings me to the next vital chapter in this journey: Brotherhood, Business, and the BPM Way.

Closing Reflection: Together, New York, Durham, and Atlanta form a sacred triangle of Black resilience, creativity, and economic power. Each city, with its own rhythm and roots, has offered us more than stages—they've given us soil to plant something enduring. From the global energy of Harlem to the historic heartbeat of Durham and the unapologetic ambition of Atlanta, Black Wall Street lives, breathes, and evolves. This chapter isn't just about places—it's about the people who dared to dream, who built in the face of adversity, and who continue to light the path forward. And as we move to the next chapter, we carry their fire with us—because the movement isn't finished. It's just getting started.

CHAPTER 13

BROTHERHOOD, BUSINESS & THE BPM WAY

The strength of Black Professional Men, Inc. (BPM) isn't measured by titles or awards. It's not even about the high-profile positions held by its members, many of whom now lead airports, launch businesses, and shape public policy. The real power of BPM is rooted in its mission: developing young Black men's minds—one scholarship, one conversation, one mentor at a time.

This is the story of a brotherhood born not from ego, but from purpose.

From Whitelock to the World

My brother, Ricky Smith, now runs Hartsfield-Jackson Atlanta International Airport—the busiest airport in the world. That achievement alone deserves national headlines. But those who know Ricky understand this moment was decades in the making. From his beginnings in West Baltimore's Whitelock community to executive leadership roles in aviation, Ricky never lost sight of his roots or the village that believed in him.

We both grew up in a community that demanded excellence despite the odds. At the heart of that village stood BPM—a circle of high standards and higher hopes.

Answering the Mayor's Call

Baltimore Mayor Kurt L. Schmoke convened a select group of promising Black men with a charge: organize, uplift the next generation, and set a standard. The call was answered by leaders like N. Scott Phillips, Drew Hawkins, and Ricky Smith—men who dreamed big and planned long. Their legacy, Black Professional Men, Inc., is a purpose-driven vehicle built for endurance.

What began locally has become a model worthy of replication in cities across the country.

Why BPM Matters

Every year, BPM awards scholarships to talented young men, but the real gift isn't the check—it's the ongoing commitment. It's the calls from mentors like Rod Carter. It's the example set by men like Edwin Avent, Omar Muhammad, and the late

Robert "Bob" Ingram, who show up when it counts.

BPM understands what our community cannot afford to forget: talent needs structure. Genius needs guidance. Potential requires protection.

Ricky's Rise Is Our Rise

Ricky's leadership at ATL is more than a personal triumph—it's a collective win for every young man who walked through BPM's doors, every scholarship recipient, and every boy on the block wondering if his life can reach beyond the corner.

From BWI to Cleveland, Ricky's leadership has centered on Black business inclusion and economic access. He didn't just speak about equity—he practiced it. His career is a living sermon; his resume, a testament to what happens when preparation meets purpose backed by community support.

The Lesson Is Clear

Movements never grow alone. Every great leader—whether Garvey, Tubman, or today's emerging kings—needs a movement, a network, a brotherhood to carry the work forward. Brotherhood is not a luxury; it is a lifeline.

BPM lives this truth. When Black men unite with integrity, consistency, and love for their people, their impact becomes unstoppable—not just for themselves, but for generations to come.

If you're wondering how to change the narrative or protect our sons in a system that often overlooks them, look no further. Organizations like BPM—and leaders like Ricky—are not just important; they are sacred.

What's Next?

We don't need saviors. We need structure. Not handouts, but hands raised in support. Not dreams alone, but decisive action.

Let's follow the BPM blueprint forged decades ago—and keep building.

As we confront the hard truths and complex challenges ahead—from economic equity to the urgent conversation on reparations—let BPM's legacy be our guide.

The journey continues. The next chapter is calling us to rise and meet it head-on.

Closing Reflection: Brotherhood, Business & the BPM Way

The true power of Black Professional Men, Inc. lies not in titles or accolades, but in its unwavering commitment to lifting up the minds, spirits, and futures of young Black men. BPM teaches us that success is never a solo journey—it's a collective rise rooted in mentorship, community, and steadfast dedication.

Ricky Smith's journey from West Baltimore to leading the world's busiest airport is more than a personal achievement. It's proof that when preparation meets community support, barriers fall and doors open wide. BPM reminds us that talent alone is not enough; it requires structure, guidance, and a brotherhood that shows up, time and again.

As we face the challenges ahead—from economic justice to the vital conversation on reparations—let BPM's legacy serve as a blueprint. We don't need saviors; we need networks strengthened, hands extended, and bold action taken. This is how we protect our sons, rewrite our story, and build a future worthy of those who paved the way.

The path forward is clear. Together, with purpose and unity, we rise.

CHAPTER 14

FEAR, POWER, AND THE PRICE OF REPARATIONS

We the black people assembled in Detroit, Michigan for the National Black Economic Development Conference are fully aware that we have been forced to come together because racist white America has exploited our resources, our minds, our bodies, our labor. For centuries we have been forced to live as colonized people inside the United States, victimized by the most vicious, racist system in the world. We have helped to build the most industrial country in the world. – James Foreman "Black Manifesto". The New York Review of Books. 10 July 1969.

It is so interesting that as I am researching and writing on strategizing Black economic wealth and power in the United States for my next book, this particular day – Monday, May 19, 2025 – is Malcolm X's 100th birthday. Honestly, it wasn't the first thing on my mind today. What's on my mind is presenting the very best manuscript I can muster to bring light, clarity, and solutions to the dilemmas facing my community.

In fact, a part of this struggle is a very important topic we, as a people, are often afraid to have. Last week, Maryland's first Black governor — and the only Black governor in the nation — vetoed a Reparations Commission bill. The bill would have established a formal process to examine the historic and ongoing inequities experienced by African descendants in Maryland. Instead, it was struck down — by a man many of us once believed might lead the charge for justice.

The Letter That Changed the Conversation

In the wake of that decision, a public letter emerged from none other than Larry S. Gibson — legal scholar, political strategist, and longtime advisor to Governor Wes Moore. Gibson urged the governor to veto the bill, calling it "redundant, distracting, and too little, too late." He framed it as a stall tactic and argued that Maryland didn't need "another two years of study." Instead, he said, the state should just act — invest in housing, education, healthcare, and minority business without using the word "reparations."

On paper, his words were assertive. Action-oriented. Even urgent. But underneath, they struck a very different chord with those of us paying close attention.

For many, this wasn't a call to action — it was a call to avoid accountability.

Gibson's logic seemed tailored not only to deflate the reparations movement in Maryland, but to **protect Governor Moore's national political image** — one that must appeal to white moderates if he has any hope of becoming a future presidential contender. The word "reparations" carries political heat, and vetoing a commission before it even began its work allowed Moore to sidestep that heat before it got any brighter.

But we have to be honest: this wasn't just politics. It was fear. And that's where the deeper story begins.

Dr. Ray Winbush: "Tell Me What You're Afraid Of"

In an interview I conducted with Dr. Ray Winbush — one of the nation's leading scholars on reparations — he didn't mince words about the veto or about Gibson's letter.

"Some in the Maryland General Assembly actually wanted our group to lead the study," he said. "But it's not just about lynching. It's about land theft, unresolved murders, Black families stolen from their communities in Baltimore. That bill was meant to examine all of that — not just history, but harm. They missed the entire point of reparations."

He paused.

"If the veto position was meant to avoid responsibility, that was cowardly."

Winbush's disappointment wasn't just about the veto. It was about how easily some of our own leaders use strategy to mask fear.

"Jews deserve reparations. Japanese Americans deserve reparations. Native people deserve reparations. But we, as Black people, are the only group where some of us argue we **don't** deserve them," he told me. "Japanese Americans don't question reparations. Neither Native Americans nor Jewish people. Our hesitation is rooted in something deeper — self-hatred, denial of reality, and most of all, a denial of history."

His words hit hard.

"Disappointment is part of the reparations struggle," Winbush said. "But it's clear the Governor does **not** fully understand reparations as they relate to Maryland. Reparations is **not** a handout — it is justice. And we need people who are brave enough to say that out loud."

He invoked the late Dr. Frances Cress Welsing:

"We need a national convention on Black fear — with no white people and no press. Just us. So we can name the fear we carry. So instead of opposing reparations, someone can finally say: *'I'm afraid I'll lose the white vote.'* That would be more honest. Say what you're afraid of. Don't deflect. Don't sabotage. Just be real."

Winbush concluded with something that should haunt every elected Black official in America:

"The only state in the country with a Black governor just voted down reparations. What kind of message does that send to the rest of the country?"

Between Political Realism and Moral Courage

This is where the conversation must go next. Because both Gibson and Winbush are elder statesmen — each with decades of service to our people. But only one, in this moment, is showing the kind of clarity this historical juncture demands.

Gibson is the seasoned insider. The tactician. The power broker who understands how politics works in white spaces. He's playing a long game, and he knows that words like "reparations" can make powerful enemies.

But Winbush is the historian. The truth-teller. The one who refuses to sell justice for strategy, or to water down the word for the sake of electoral viability.

Between them lies the challenge of our generation: How do we **gain power** without abandoning truth? How do we win elections without erasing our history? How do we move forward **without betraying the people who brought us this far**?

Closing Reflection: The Real Test of Leadership

Leadership isn't measured by convenience or silence—it's tested in moments that demand courage and conviction. Governor Moore's choice to veto a critical conversation about Maryland's legacy of slavery and Jim Crow wasn't just a political decision—it was a moral crossroads. History will judge not only what leaders do but what they refuse to do.

True progress in building Black wealth and power requires facing our history head-on, no matter how uncomfortable it makes others. We cannot prioritize white discomfort over Black visibility and justice. Silence is not strength—it's surrender.

As Malcolm X challenged us, if we're not willing to risk everything for freedom, then the word itself loses meaning. On the centennial of his birth, that call echoes louder than ever: leadership demands bravery, honesty, and an unflinching commitment to legacy over lip service.

The real test is not just in words, but in action—and the time to act is now.

CHAPTER 15

LEGACY OVER LIP SERVICE

Reparations are a necessary part of the American story. It is a debt owed. Yet whether they come or not, we must never forget — Black people in America have already built empires, businesses, towns, movements, and legacies. The ancestors were never waiting for a government check.

We must also remember that our strength as a people has never rested in the hands of any president, political party, or elected official — including those who look like us.

Let's pause to acknowledge a few giants whose names are too often forgotten:

1. **Maggie Lena Walker** was the first woman (of any race) in America to charter and preside over a bank. In Jim Crow Virginia, she taught Black women self-sufficiency, ran a newspaper, and helped create the financial infrastructure for an entire community.

2. **Charles R. Patterson**, a formerly enslaved Black man, bought out a white carriage business, rebranded it, and built the *C.R. Patterson & Sons* Company — the first and only Black-owned automobile manufacturer in the U.S. He did this before Ford took over the car industry.

3. **Annie Turnbo Malone**, a chemist and entrepreneur, built a beauty empire that trained thousands of Black women (including Madam C.J. Walker) and established one of the first major Black-owned corporations in America.

4. **William Leidesdorff**, a wealthy businessman of African and Jewish descent, helped establish San Francisco's first school and became a major power broker in early California.

5. And **Chief John Horse**, a maroon and military leader, led hundreds of Black Seminoles from enslavement in Florida to refuge in Mexico — defeating slave catchers and U.S. troops along the way.

These weren't anomalies. These were **blueprints**. Every one of them faced legal, financial, and racial terror — yet they still built. Not because they were superhuman, but because they were clear.

They understood power.

Closing Reflection: What's Power?

Power isn't handed over lightly—it demands to be claimed and fought for, just as Frederick Douglass warned us. True power doesn't live in titles or fancy offices; it lives in the courage to stand unapologetically for our people, even when it's uncomfortable or inconvenient. Too often, those placed in positions of influence have forgotten this truth. They were taught to conform, to control, to silence, and to prioritize appearances over action. But the Black community sees through the smoke and mirrors. We know the difference between empty gestures and real change. Between speeches that soothe and protests that shake the foundations. Between leaders who show up for a photo op and those who show up when it counts.

The streets are watching. Our youth are watching. And they're asking the question that can no longer be ignored: Where were you when it mattered?

If we are to move beyond the shadow of Civil Rights mode, we must embrace a new era of leadership—one rooted in accountability, courage, and unwavering commitment to the liberation and uplift of our communities. It's time to stop performing and start building. The time for real power is now.

CHAPTER 16

STILL IN CIVIL RIGHTS MODE

I am so tired of Black people who do not believe in Black people.

Has America contaminated our self-worth that much? We read Black history books about W.E.B. DuBois, Marcus Garvey, Ida B. Wells, Fannie Lou Hamer, Harriet Tubman, Frederick Douglass—the list goes on. None of them made it into the history books by being scared. Fannie Lou took beatings many men couldn't endure, simply because she refused to bow to racism. She never surrendered her dignity. That's the kind of courage we've lost.

Today, too many of us have traded in that fire. We're scared of losing a car note or a mortgage payment. We've sold our souls for comfort and a couple coins. And we wonder why our children don't respect us? Is there really any wonder? We've failed them. We've bowed to fear, while mass incarceration explodes, Black businesses struggle to stay afloat, and our communities fall further behind.

What happened to us?

In a conversation with Erich March, CEO of King Memorial Park and part of the legendary March Funeral Home legacy, he pointed to a turning point: the Vietnam War. Twenty percent of the soldiers were Black, and many came home with drug addictions. At the same time, cocaine and heroin swept into our neighborhoods. Families shattered. Fathers disappeared. PTSD went untreated. Our foundation cracked.

There was a time when we may have been better off segregated, because at least back then, we knew we had to fight. But when we moved into suburban cul-de-sacs and whispered words like "progress," we forgot that the struggle wasn't over. We became too comfortable.

And then, I had a conversation with Attorney Robert Dashiell, a longtime member of our Political Roundtable on *BlackUSA.News*. His words cut deep.

On the topic of reparations, he didn't just talk about stolen labor. He talked about stolen potential.

"They didn't just take our labor," he said. "They took our intellectual property. Our inventions. You like your cell phone? GPS? Black minds made that possible. Hell, a Black man even gave them Jack Daniels. So no, this ain't just about unpaid work. That's bad enough. But it goes deeper."

It's not just theft. It's annihilation. Systematic destruction.

"They stole our ability to create systems. And when we prove we can build those systems without them—what happens? This country bombs us.

Don't forget, there are only two times the U.S. dropped bombs on its own citizens:

Tulsa's Greenwood District.
Philadelphia's MOVE Movement.

When we stand on our own, they try to erase us."

And that erasure starts early—with our children.

"We tell our kids to go to school. But what's left for them there?

We stripped the schools bare. Took away gym. Took away art. Took away Home Ec. Took away shop.

Music? Gone. Choir? Gone. Band? Gone.

All the things that could spark something in their spirit—we erased it.

Then we act surprised when they're angry, unmotivated, and disconnected."

We are asking our children to dream inside buildings built to break them.

"And we teach them—without even saying it—that whatever someone else has is better than what we can give. Then we wonder why they don't respect us?

C'mon, man. I'm sick of this shit."

Then came the line that stuck with me the most:

"We're still stuck in Civil Rights mode. But if we're honest, the end result of that movement—and the agenda pushed by Donald Trump and Elon Musk—ends in the same damn place: Black invisibility.

The Civil Rights folks called it assimilation.

Trump and Musk? They just say it louder:

'You're not here. We don't see you. We don't have to acknowledge you.'

Same difference.

How the hell am I supposed to assimilate into a white world that still looks at me and sees nothing but Black?

Our ancestors are crying in the grave."

This chapter is a wake-up call—a refusal to let the memory of our ancestors be reduced to history books while their dreams die in our silence. It's a reminder that the fight didn't end with the Civil Rights Movement—it merely changed its shape. From economic theft to educational erasure, from quiet assimilation to overt invisibility, from Civil Rights to Silver Rights (in the words of Ray Haysbert), the struggle for Black dignity is far from over. If we are to honor those who came before us, we must confront the systems that still seek to erase us and reclaim the fire we've been taught to fear. The time for passive hope is over. Now is the time for active, unapologetic reawakening.

Closing Reflection:

This wasn't just a conversation. It was a reckoning.

A reminder that progress without truth is performance. That invisibility—whether through bombs, broken schools, or polite assimilation—is not freedom. That if we're still asking to be seen in 2025, the movement isn't over. It's just been muted.

And we, the descendants of giants, must unmute it.

We must stand, unapologetically, on our Blackness—ready to reclaim, rebuild, and reimagine what's possible.

CHAPTER 17

WE KNOW WHAT TIME IT IS

We've seen the betrayal up close. We've watched gatekeepers hoard access, sell influence, and sabotage the next generation to stay relevant. And we've seen brilliant elders pushed to the margins, dismissed for being "too radical," while the real radicals run the boardrooms that extract from our communities daily.

If this hits hard, good. It's supposed to.

This isn't bitterness. This is clarity.

We have always been powerful. We have always been strategic. And we have always known how to move — with or without permission.

The only question now is:

What will we build next — and who's coming with us?

STEM City USA: Dr. Tyrone Taborn

When it comes to visionaries of the digital frontier, there is no one quite like Dr. Tyrone Taborn.

He is a one-man hurricane in the Metaverse — a force of intellect, strategy, and unapologetic advocacy. For more than 40 years, Dr. Taborn has been fighting the good fight: closing the digital divide, championing equity in technology, and speaking boldly against what he aptly calls *digital apartheid*. His mission? To ensure Black and brown communities aren't just consumers of technology, but creators and leaders in the digital economy.

If you know him, you know this — he doesn't stop. He *can't* stop. Even if he wanted to retire, the man isn't wired to sit still. As long as there's a keyboard and a Wi-Fi signal, Tyrone Taborn is launching ships into the 21st century and beyond.

Born in Chicago in 1959 and raised in a Black and Latino household in Los Angeles, he's always embodied the bridge between cultures and industries. Maybe it's because he spent his childhood summers in Tulsa, Oklahoma. At Cornell University, he was selected as a Lyndon B. Johnson intern for Congressman Julian C. Dixon, and inducted into the prestigious Quill and Dagger

Society. Even then, he was a standout — a scholar with deep purpose and immense potential.

But it's what he built after that truly changed the game.

In 1986, Dr. Taborn founded Career Communications Group, a multimillion-dollar talent development and publishing enterprise. Through it, he launched *U.S. Black Engineer & Information Technology*, still the nation's only general-interest tech magazine for African Americans. He's also the brain behind *Hispanic Engineer* magazine and the award-winning TV show *Success Through Education*.

His annual BEYA (Black Engineer of the Year Awards) Conference is nothing short of legendary. For four decades, BEYA has opened doors for thousands of students of color to engage with leaders from top tech companies, federal agencies, and the military. I've seen it firsthand — from the grand exhibits to the U.S. military's unforgettable displays. BEYA isn't just an event. It's a launchpad for generations of future engineers, coders, and innovators.

But what I admire most about Dr. Taborn is this: for all his global reach and high-level access — and trust me, the man knows generals, prime ministers, and CEOs — he has never forgotten where he came from. He's never turned his back on the inner city. In fact, he's doubled down on it.

Today, STEM City USA is headquartered in West Baltimore at Dr. Al Hathaway's new $15 million Thurgood Marshall Amenity Center. It sits on sacred ground near historic Druid Hill Avenue — among the legacy churches like Bethel A.M.E. Zion, Sharp Street, and Union Baptist — and close to the same streets that raised the Mitchell family and other Baltimore giants. That center is breathtaking inside. It's a bright light in a place that has long deserved investment and care. And thanks to Taborn, technology, innovation, and opportunity now have a permanent home in the heart of our community.

His work isn't about flash — it's about future.

He is also the founder of Black Family Technology Week, La Familia Technology Awareness Week, and the Native American Technology Awareness Project — all dedicated to bringing awareness and access to communities too often left behind in the tech space. His civic engagement is extensive: he's served on the boards of Morgan State, the

Baltimore Urban League, the *Afro-American Newspaper*, and countless others.

He's received numerous accolades, from a Congressional Black Caucus honor to being named one of the 50 Most Important African Americans in Technology by *BlackMoney.com*. In 2005, he was awarded an honorary doctorate from Morgan State University.

Dr. Tyrone Taborn is a publisher, a civic leader, a digital pioneer, and a relentless advocate. He's also a husband, a father, and a mentor to many, including myself. CCG is my largest supporter to date. This man believes in the work we do, and that is priceless. He understands my father's favorite saying, "With a closed hand, nothing gets in and nothing gets out. With an open hand, there are endless possibilities. The moral to the story: Help somebody."

But above all, he is proof that one person — with vision, conviction, and a keyboard — can truly change the world. Dr. Taborn's story reminds us of the power of vision and influence on a grand scale. But the values that truly ground me — the ones that shaped my sense of purpose — come from someone even closer: my mother.

Closing Reflection:

We're not confused. We know what time it is. This moment calls for clarity, conviction, and courage. No more waiting for permission. No more begging for inclusion. The blueprint is in our hands, and the examples — like Dr. Tyrone Taborn — prove that we already have what it takes to lead, build, and transform. The question isn't whether we're ready. The question is whether we're willing to honor the legacy, invest in each other, and move like we know who we are. Because when we do, there's no gatekeeper, no system, no silence that can stop us. The future isn't coming — it's already here. And it's ours to shape.

CHAPTER 18

ON MY MOTHER: A WORD ON WEALTH

My mother, Lillie Juanita Glover, was born on the 4th of July — and she lived up to the date. She was a firecracker: fierce, focused, and full of purpose. She raised four children, and I was her last — and my father's first and only. She had three unshakable rules for all of us:

1. At 18, you're leaving — college, military, or work, but you're out.

2. Don't bring any babies home in the meantime.

3. Own your house.

Simple. Firm. And effective. She batted 4-for-4.

Now, I've heard some folks say 18 is too early to leave home. To that, I say — take it up with Lillie in heaven. She believed — and so do I — that if you raise your children right, you instill in them the confidence, skills, and grit to step into adulthood fully equipped. She started preparing me for that departure as early as 15. When she passed during my second year at Morehouse, it was one of the hardest moments of my life. But I was ready. She made sure of it.

By age 27, I began buying the home I live in — directly from my father. By 37, it was fully paid off. I've blown a lot of money in my lifetime, no doubt, but buying a house was one of the best decisions I've ever made.

Think about it: what many people pay in rent each month could easily cover a mortgage. The real difference comes down to three things:

1. Credit

2. A down payment

3. The willingness to follow the process

Buying my home not only gave me a foundation — it gave me freedom. It allowed me to build my business without worrying about rent or a landlord. That kind of security is priceless, especially for entrepreneurs.

In fact, one of the smartest financial moves I made in business was to keep overhead low. I realized I didn't need a fancy office — just a business address. My good friend, William Hopson of Icetech, Inc., made that possible for me for over 15 years. And let me be honest — I didn't need an office to impress anybody. For what? To stunt? That's ego. Wealth isn't loud.

Let me say this clearly:

The single most significant financial move most people can make is to buy a home.

Not just to live in — but to build stability, equity, and legacy. With intention and planning, it's possible. And it's powerful.

If you want to build wealth — start with your foundation. Own it.

Final Word: Own the Future

We've traveled through history, policy, pain, and power — through Black Wall Streets built and burned, through systems designed to hold us back, and strategies created to move us forward. But the real question is: **What will you build?**

If there's one thing my mother, Lillie Juanita Glover, taught me — it's this: **you prepare your children to stand, not to settle.** You show them how to walk with dignity, speak with purpose, and build something that lasts. Whether that's a business, a home, or a community — the point is to **own it**.

Because ownership is power.

You don't need permission to change your future. You need a plan. You need discipline. You need faith — in yourself, in your people, and in the God who has carried us this far.

We can't keep waiting for someone else to come save our communities. We are the cavalry. We are the strategy. And we are the solution.

So build it. Buy it. Own it. And leave something behind.

Our ancestors left us a blueprint. Now it's our time to draw up the next version.

Let's get to work.

Reflection: Own Something You Can Pass Down

Rent pays the landlord. Ownership builds legacy. My mother didn't just tell me to buy a house — she handed me a blueprint for independence. Homeownership gave me peace of mind when business got slow. It gave me stability when life got shaky. And it gave me something to leave behind.

You don't have to start with much — just start with a plan. And when you do buy, buy smart. Buy like it matters. Because it does. **When we own, we build. When we build, we rise.**

From the foundation of ownership, we now look ahead to how Black empowerment is expanding and evolving.

CHAPTER 19

WHAT'S NEXT – BUILDING THE FUTURE OF BLACK EMPOWERMENT

"If Tulsa was the model, today's version is digital, decentralized, and diaspora-driven."

Welcome to the New Black Renaissance

The 21st-century Black Wall Street is no longer confined to a single neighborhood or city. It's digital, decentralized, and vibrantly global. Leading the charge are visionaries like Dr. Tyrone Taborn—but they're joined by a growing network of tech innovators, entrepreneurs, legal advocates, and brand builders who are redefining Black empowerment for a new era.

Take Mandy Bowman, founder and CEO of **Official Black Wall Street (OBWS)**, a revolutionary mobile app that connects consumers to Black-owned businesses across the country. Born from Bowman's response to the gentrification that wiped out Black businesses in her Brooklyn neighborhood, OBWS now serves as a vital digital lifeline for emerging entrepreneurs nationwide. Inspired by Tulsa's legacy, Bowman designed OBWS as both tribute and tool—aimed at building wealth, visibility, and sustainability in the Black community. Though early funding was a challenge, requiring a Kickstarter campaign to launch, OBWS is now scaling rapidly with major updates and a forthcoming seed round, fueling the national #BuyBlack movement.

But the New Renaissance extends far beyond business—it's powered by formidable legal champions like **Damario Solomon-Simmons, Esq., M.Ed.**, a nationally recognized civil rights attorney based in Oklahoma. As founder and Executive Director of **Justice for Greenwood**, Solomon-Simmons leads efforts to secure reparations and justice for survivors and descendants of the 1921 Tulsa Race Massacre. His work combines legal advocacy, public education, and community engagement to address systemic disparities in health, education, real estate, and business. A seasoned litigator with nearly two decades of experience, Solomon-Simmons also manages a law firm specializing in civil litigation, employment law, government relations, and entertainment law.

Looking at the power of public relations, **Dr. Pam Perry**, an award-winning communications strategist from Detroit, helps entrepreneurs and experts craft compelling narratives that convert into media visibility and revenue. Founder of Pam Perry PR and publisher of *Speakers Magazine*, she's guided clients to major features on CNN, *Oprah Magazine, Essence,* and more. Known as a "PR Guru," Dr. Perry's specialty is helping clients "brand—and get paid—like superstars."

Chicago's **Cynthia Boykin**, known as "The Master Networker," builds bridges across industries with her consultancy, **What U Need Is....** Her platform connects over 56,000 professionals spanning fashion, film, publishing, entertainment, and design, opening doors for businesses far beyond Chicago. Recognized nationally for her leadership and impact, Cynthia excels at aligning the right people at the right time—whether on stage, mentoring entrepreneurs, or closing deals behind the scenes.

In journalism, **Cheryl Smith** stands as a titan of the Black press. With over 40 years of experience, she leads the *I Messenger Media Group*, which publishes influential outlets like *Texas Metro News* and *Garland Journal*. Beyond publishing, Cheryl hosts

Cheryl's World on Blog Talk Radio and serves as Secretary of the National Association of Black Journalists and Regional President of the National Newspaper Publishers Association. A passionate educator and advocate, Cheryl's career reflects an unwavering commitment to truth and community empowerment.

Cheryl Thompson-Morton is a visionary driving journalism equity and innovation. As Head of Advisory Programs at the Lenfest Institute for Journalism, she has championed Black-owned media through training, research, and funding initiatives. Previously, as Director of the Black Media Initiative at the Craig Newmark Graduate School of Journalism, Cheryl brought BMORENews.com into a national network of Black media outlets. A Drexel University summa cum laude graduate, Cheryl combines strategic insight with a deep commitment to equity, shaping a thriving future for Black journalism.

From the Biden White House, **Rodericka Applewhaite** served as Director of Black Media, expanding access for Black journalists and media outlets to the White House press corps. She helped elevate voices often overlooked by mainstream media and fostered emerging Black correspondents who tell their communities' stories on a national platform. Though no longer in the role, her legacy continues to inspire greater media equity.

Finally, **Carl Brown**, State/Executive Director of the District of Columbia Small Business Development Center at Howard University, has hosted multiple Black Wall Street events that uplift Black entrepreneurs. With over 25 years of experience spanning telecommunications, consumer goods, and public sector roles, Carl is a trusted voice on economic development, hosting "The Small Business Report" on Sirius XM and producing impactful business media content.

If there's one lesson I've learned from working with Walter Edwards and Regina Smith in Harlem on the Black Economic Empowerment Commission, it's this: **collaboration is everything**. We're only as strong as our networks. My advice? Build your network—one person at a time.

Whether it's Pam Perry in Detroit, Cynthia Boykin in Chicago, or Cheryl Smith in Dallas-Fort Worth, we all need to connect with like-minded leaders. For me, that means collaborating with Cheryl Thompson-Morton in Philadelphia, who recognized *BMORENews.com* and *BlackUSA.News* on her national map of Black media. Or partnering with Rodericka Applewhaite, New York native Mandy Bowman, Oklahoma's Damario Solomon-Simmons, and Washington, D.C.'s Carl Brown. These are the dedicated, skilled leaders I have the privilege to work with daily. They love what they do—and they excel at it.

This is the new Black Wall Street.

CHAPTER 20

THE QUIET POWERHOUSE: WHAT THE FUNERAL BUSINESS TAUGHT ME ABOUT BLACK ECONOMICS

As we celebrate this vibrant, decentralized renaissance of Black innovation—from tech apps to legal advocacy to transformative media—I'm reminded that Black empowerment is not new. While today's pioneers push boundaries globally, our foundation was laid long ago by everyday heroes in local communities. Before the digital economy, there was the neighborhood economy. Before social media, there were social pillars—like barbers, beauticians, and funeral directors—who quietly built the backbone of Black enterprise. And for me, one of the most formative influences on my understanding of economics and service was watching my father as a funeral director and mortician. This next chapter takes us there—not into the digital cloud, but into the community chapel, where dignity, economics, and legacy have always intertwined.

I was raised in a home where dignity met business, where service to others wasn't just a calling — it was the family business. As the son of a funeral director and mortician, I saw early on how Black-owned funeral homes were more than places of mourning. They were engines of economic activity, community leadership, and generational stability. In a world where Black businesses often fight for visibility and equity, the funeral industry quietly held us down — feeding families, employing neighbors, and modeling what self-sustained Black enterprise really looks like.

Contracts Don't Define Us

In Maryland, there is always talk — especially in the MBE community — about minority business enterprise (MBE) programs. Many Black businesses thrive in this arena, which includes federal, state, and local government contracts. It's a vital lane for some, especially those with goods and services that align with government needs.

I remember a younger MBE advocate once came on my show. We ended up talking past each other more than actually listening. It was one of those conversations where passions rise, perspectives clash, and even though it made for compelling radio, I walked away knowing I had a responsibility to clear the air. As the elder, I had to do my part to make things right. Baltimore is too small, and our community too interconnected, for division. We have enough of that already.

The young advocate argued that our MBEs are floundering. And truthfully, from one vantage point — particularly within MBE contract data — he's right. Black MBEs only get a sliver of the pie. The majority of contracts still go to white-owned firms.

But here's what I needed to say: not all Black businesses are dependent on contracts. In fact, many of us are doing well without them. We're not floundering — we're flourishing. Quietly. Consistently. We hold down Black families every single day. Our existence isn't validated by state spreadsheets or federal bids. It's validated by our impact.

A Legacy of Service and Self-Sufficiency

I speak now as the son of a funeral director and mortician who served as President of the Funeral Directors and Morticians Association of Maryland. Having grown up in the industry, I saw firsthand how this community helped build our community.

A Christian funeral isn't just a ceremony — it's an economic web. There's the beautician (if the deceased is a woman), the hearse, the drivers, the church fee, the preacher's honorarium, the cemetery costs. Someone washes the limousines. Someone handles the phones. Someone coordinates the services. That funeral pays a lot of people. And often, they're all from the neighborhood.

The Black funeral business has long been a self-contained ecosystem — hiring from within, circulating dollars locally, and providing stable, respected employment in our communities. It's a quiet powerhouse.

The Forgotten Power of Black Institutions

In Sandtown, we had George G. Kelson Elementary School. Mr. Kelson owned a funeral home on Calhoun Street, eventually succeeded by Vernon Bailey. I imagine they named the school after him because of his service to the community.

When I think of March Funeral Homes in Baltimore, I think of William and Roberta March. They didn't just run a business — they built an institution. Their name carries weight not just because of wealth, but because of the dignity, care, and community support they extended for generations.

These businesses were more than storefronts — they were anchors. Places of strength, trust, and example. In a time when Black institutions are under threat or disappearing altogether, these families and their enterprises show us what enduring Black leadership looks like.

Mutual Respect is the Real Currency

We have to get back to a basic level of self-respect and mutual respect. The custodian is just as important as the president. Everyone puts their pants on the same way. When we elevate ourselves above others because of income, status, or position, resentment follows. Bet on it.

But when we treat each other with respect, that foolishness fades. Real leaders don't lead with ego. They lead with service. That's what I saw growing up. That's what I believe Black Wall Street was about: us helping us.

Black Wall Street Starts at Home

We've been taught to measure success by outside approval—by contracts secured, seats offered at tables we didn't build. But what if we remembered that we've *always* built our own?

Funeral homes. Barbershops. Corner stores. Daycare centers. These aren't footnotes in our story. They *are* the story. These are our original Black Wall Streets—places where legacy, service, and community came together to create wealth that could be seen, touched, and passed on.

Real Black wealth isn't flashy. It's rooted. It honors our elders, supports our neighbors, and builds for the next generation. We don't need permission to prosper. We've had the blueprint all along. *We are the infrastructure we've been waiting for.*

And yet, even as I came to appreciate the power of local Black institutions, something deeper stirred within me—something ancestral. The funeral home taught me about legacy and economic strength. But a missing piece remained: Africa.

Not the Africa found in textbooks or newsfeeds. The real one. The one buried in my bloodline. The one that whispered to me in moments of quiet, asking, *When are you coming home?*

Before we talk about where we're going, we must first honor where we come from. Our ancestors built thriving communities in places like Sandtown with dignity, vision, and resilience. That same spirit extends beyond city blocks and state lines. My journey took me from the streets of Baltimore to the soil of Africa—and in doing so, redefined not only who I was, but why I'm here.

As a journalist. As a businessman. As a servant of the people.

Closing Reflection: The Blueprint Was Always Ours

The funeral home taught me that real power isn't loud—it's loyal. It shows up early, stays late, and serves without applause. It buries our dead with dignity and lifts our living with jobs, compassion, and care. I didn't need a Harvard case study to understand Black economics. I lived in one.

We talk about ecosystems now like they're new. But long before the buzzwords, we had our own—rooted in service, fueled by trust, and grounded in community. These weren't temporary programs or trend-driven startups. They were sacred institutions. And they worked.

What I learned as the son of a mortician was simple but profound: **Black enterprise isn't a hustle—it's**

a heritage. It's built not just on margins, but on meaning. Not just for profit, but for people.

Hence, while we scale into digital platforms and global partnerships, let us not forget the quiet powerhouses that got us here. The barbers who mentored. The beauticians who prayed. The funeral directors who comforted and employed. They weren't just doing business. They were doing ministry.

And they left us a blueprint: **serve first, own something, hire your people, and treat every transaction like a trust.**

In this next era of Black renaissance—tech, media, trade, law—let's not just go forward. Let's go forward *rooted*. Let's take the best of what we've inherited and build with intention. Because legacy is not what we leave behind. It's what we build while we're here. And **Joey Brown**, successor to his father's Joseph C. Brown Funeral Home, is the pristine example. He is the first and only Black funeral director in Baltimore who built his own crematory. And if that is not revolutionary enough for you, then also note that he is the first person in Maryland to construct what is called a "water cremation" system utilizing alkaline hydrolysis for what he has tagged as a "cleaner, greener, kinder, and gentler" form of cremation.

And as for me? I carry the casket and the camera. The pen and the passport. Because from Baltimore to Benin, I now know exactly who I am—and what I'm here to do.

CHAPTER 21

A JOURNEY TO AFRICA: FROM JORDAN TO ADDIS ABABA

It was September 2002. I was traveling with Arthur Murphy and eight other Black journalists from across the U.S. on a 10-day familiarization tour. Arthur, who had fallen in love with Jordan during his college days, had been taking journalists to the region for years. What made this trip especially intense was its timing — we were there just as the U.S. began its invasion of Iraq. In other words, we were in what could be considered a kidnap zone.

We were headed south, driving through Aqaba. As we prepared to make a right turn, someone suddenly exclaimed, "And that's Egypt!" I was stunned. Silly me — I knew we were close, but I had no idea we were *that* close. I hadn't expected to see Africa on that trip, and yet, there she was — right before my eyes. I broke down and cried for 45 minutes.

To my fellow journalists, I said something that had been living in my spirit for years: "I haven't seen my mother in 400 years." That's what it felt like.

When we arrived at the hotel, the first thing I did was call home. I told my father and then-wife what I had just experienced — that I had *seen* Africa with my own eyes.

Four years later, after many years of longing and spiritual preparation, I boarded Ethiopian Airlines — the oldest airline in Africa — and flew to Ethiopia. Of all places I could have landed first, it was Addis Ababa. Divine intervention, no doubt. To set foot in the only African nation never colonized still blows my mind. It wasn't just a journey across continents. It was a journey through history, identity, and spiritual alignment.

That first glimpse of Africa, and later, my first steps on Ethiopian soil, marked the beginning of a lifelong commitment — to reconnect, to uplift, and to share her story with the world.

CHAPTER 22

BMORENEWS AND THE UNITED NATIONS: WHERE IT ALL COMES TOGETHER

Of all the places this journey has taken me—from the deserts of Jordan to the mountains of Ethiopia, and even to the halls of the White House to cover topics like HBCUs, HIV/AIDS, and the U.S. Black Chambers of Commerce—few experiences have matched the profound honor of being invited to the Black Publishers and Media Executives Global Forum on Africa at the United Nations. That invitation came from the late, great Bob Ingram, a cherished mentor, friend, and longtime supporter of my work.

That day—November 22, 2011—was unforgettable. I was in Harlem, thanks to my dear friend Marsha Reeves Jews, who ensured I made the journey and returned home safely, with more knowledge than I left with. The Forum was life-changing, not just because of the powerful speakers or the impressive setting, but because of what it represented: a convergence of my passions—media, Black empowerment, international development, Pan-

African unity, and economic cooperation across the Diaspora.

When Bob Ingram sent that email inviting me to the United Nations, my heart swelled with gratitude. It was a moment of validation. After nearly two decades in journalism—starting with the *Sandtown-Winchester ViewPoint* and moving into radio, television, and the founding of *BMORENEWS*—this was one of the highest honors I had received. Bob saw something in me: the international lens, the unapologetic Black voice, the commitment to truth-telling in our community.

Bob wasn't just a publisher. He was the publisher of *Uptown Professional Magazine*, a strategic thinker, a truth-bearer, and someone who knew the value of elevating Black media voices. He believed we deserved seats at global tables—and that we should bring our audience with us.

This forum felt like the fulfillment of so many pieces of my life's mission. My graduate studies at Morgan State had centered on African-African American economic cooperation, particularly focusing on Botswana. I had already visited Africa in 2006 with Global Vessels and engaged in cooperative efforts in Ethiopia and Tanzania. And now, standing inside the UN, surrounded by Black excellence, it all came full circle.

Bob said it best:

"The purpose of this Global Forum on Africa was to create a venue where Black publishers and media executives could receive unfiltered information about Africa and share it with their audiences."

He recognized what many of us in the Diaspora have long felt: that Africa is more than famine or victimhood—it's a continent rich in opportunity, culture, and promise. And we in Black media have a responsibility to tell that story.

The forum brought together powerhouse outlets like *Black Enterprise, TheRoot.com,* and leaders like Roland Rich of the UN Office for Partnerships, Dr. Josephine Ojiambo of Kenya's UN Mission, and MacDella Cooper, the dynamic Liberian philanthropist. Each voice emphasized opportunity, unity, and collaboration.

Bob also highlighted how African immigrants in the U.S. were building caucuses to support education and healthcare back home—laying the groundwork for future partnerships with African Americans in the States.

One of the Forum's co-sponsors was *The Network Journal*, led by Aziz Gueye Adetimirin, a media mogul in his own right and a brother whose life story embodies vision, hard work, and relentless dedication. An immigrant from West Africa, a U.S. Air Force veteran, and a trailblazer in digital Black media, Aziz's work continues to inspire new generations of Black entrepreneurs and publishers.

His "40 Under 40" initiative in both the U.S. and Africa is just one of many examples of his commitment to elevating excellence across the Diaspora.

Among the other attendees who left an impression was Debert Cook, publisher of *African American Golfer's Digest*. She emphasized how the forum helped shift perceptions of Africa and showcased serious investment and outsourcing opportunities on the continent. Her magazine, a certified PGA of America Diverse Supplier, has already hosted golf events in Ghana and Senegal—further proof that Africa is not just a cause, but a partner.

And then there was Marsha Jews, Baltimore's own renaissance woman and dear friend, whose connections, wisdom, and unwavering support have guided me for years. A former host of *Keep It*

Movin' on WEAA 88.9 FM, Marsha brings light wherever she goes. Her accolades—including the Mercedes Benz Vision Award and recognition in *Who's Who in Black Baltimore*—only scratch the surface of her impact.

The forum reminded me why we do this work. It reminded me of my duty—not only to my local community in Baltimore but to the global Black family. We must tell our stories. We must correct the record. We must build bridges—across neighborhoods, cities, countries, and continents.

Bob Ingram left us too soon. But his vision lives on. I carry it with me every time I publish a story, recognize an entrepreneur, or speak into a microphone. He taught me that Black media isn't just about headlines—it's about heritage, healing, and hope.

Thank you, Bob. You were more than a mentor. You were a movement.

Closing Reflection

Standing in the halls of the United Nations that day, I wasn't just a journalist—I was a vessel. A vessel for the ancestors, for the community that raised me, for the young writers still trying to find their voice, and for the countless stories that never made headlines but deserved to. That moment wasn't just a reward; it was a responsibility.

Bob Ingram saw in us the potential to shift narratives—not just about Africa, but about ourselves. He reminded us that Black media is sacred ground. It is where truth finds its wings. It's where our dignity is documented, our excellence amplified, our futures imagined.

This chapter of my life—this forum, these friendships, this global calling—made it clear: the work we do is bigger than bylines or broadcasts. It's about connecting dots between Baltimore and Botswana, Harlem and Harar, the boardrooms of Manhattan and the grassroots of West Baltimore. It's about restoring pride, reclaiming power, and rewriting what the world thinks it knows about us.

So as I move forward—still writing, still building, still fighting for the truth—I do so knowing that this journey is far from over. The mission continues. And every word I write is a brick in the bridge Bob dared us to build—one that connects the Diaspora not only in struggle, but in strength, vision, and purpose.

This is BMORENEWS. This is legacy. And this—
this is love in action.

CHAPTER 23

THE ARCHITECT OF NEW AFRICA — IBRAHIM TRAORÉ AND THE ROAD TO PAN-AFRICAN SOVEREIGNTY

If there was ever one thing my father and I disagreed on, it was Africa. He had his reasons—maybe he'd read too much, seen too much, or lived through too much disillusionment. But at age fifteen, and even more so today, I believe in the power of an independent Africa. Not just politically independent, but economically self-sufficient, culturally unified, and globally respected.

I've heard the stereotypes. I've heard African Americans talk about Africans, especially Nigerians. And I've heard some Africans' harsh takes on African Americans. But here's the thing—we both got those ideas from somewhere else. Long before we meet our melanated brothers and sisters across the Atlantic, we've already been contaminated by someone else's narrative. Usually, that "someone" is Western media.

And that is why owning our own narrative—and our own media outlets—is not optional. It's essential.

Too many of us can tell you about Dubai but have never considered Dakar. We romanticize trips to the UAE without knowing slavery was only officially abolished there in 1971. We move without asking deeper questions. So when a Black American returns from Africa and tells me how deeply they were moved, how much they learned, how at home they felt—I smile every time.

Because America has done a masterful job severing the connection between Black Americans and Africa. They've disconnected us not only from the continent, but from our global Black family—whether in the Caribbean, South America, or Europe. But the truth is, Black people are everywhere. We're global by design. If the San people of Namibia hold the oldest DNA on Earth, then we are not only the original people—we're the original travelers.

Africa is the birthplace of humanity. And yes, Africans had ships before the Vikings or Columbus. Why wouldn't they? Africa was writing history while Europe was still figuring out plumbing.

So why do so many of us still carry a Tarzan image of Africa? Why don't we know you can't drive there from America? Why are we still undereducated about the geography, history, and beauty of the continent that birthed civilization?

That's why I will always honor the late Dr. Patricia Newton, a fierce Pan-Africanist who reminded me that African Americans and continental Africans face a common enemy—and that unity is not a luxury. It's a survival strategy.

As a student of international affairs, I've studied the dynamics between the Global North and the Global South. I know the game. The wealth of the Global South has been systematically extracted for centuries—first through slavery and colonization, now through debt traps and puppet governments. The hustle has evolved, but the con remains the same.

Whether it's the exploitation of people in the streets or nations in the suites, the logic of greed still rules: "Pimpin' is pimpin'," as they say. And some of the most ruthless pimps wear suits and sit on corporate boards or lead international institutions.

Which brings me to Burkina Faso—and a man every Black person on Earth should know.

His name is **Captain Ibrahim Traoré**, and he represents a new chapter in African resistance. A bold, young leader who—at just 34 years old—rose to power in 2022 after leading Burkina Faso's second coup that year. But this isn't just another power grab. Traoré speaks a different language: sovereignty, self-determination, Pan-Africanism.

He expelled French troops. He rejected IMF and World Bank "aid." He called out neocolonialism to its face. He linked arms with Mali and Niger to form the **Alliance of Sahel States (AES)**—a new bloc of African nations fed up with foreign control and ready to forge their own path.

This isn't just politics. This is revolution.

The AES alliance has launched real, tangible projects. Chief among them: a pan-Sahel railway linking Ouagadougou (Burkina Faso), Bamako (Mali), and Niamey (Niger). This isn't about just moving people—it's about moving power. This rail project is a symbol of economic liberation. It means intra-African trade, youth mobility, regional job creation, and an escape from dependency on Western donors. And it's being built with local labor and resources—**no foreign loans, no strings attached.**

More importantly, this project challenges the legacy of colonialism: the artificial borders, the CFA franc, the foreign-imposed trade policies. It speaks directly to the dreams of African legends like Thomas Sankara and Kwame Nkrumah. And it shows us that **unity requires infrastructure, not just ideology**.

Traoré knows this isn't just about speeches. It's about building. Roads. Rail. Internet. Power grids. That's what real sovereignty looks like. That's what real Pan-Africanism demands.

Of course, there are criticisms. Burkina Faso still faces immense challenges: violent insurgencies, fragile institutions, human rights concerns. And like many populist leaders, Traoré's growing power has sparked fears of authoritarianism. But I would rather critique from within the family than have colonial powers lecture us on democracy while looting our wealth.

The bigger picture is this: Africa is no longer waiting for handouts or permission.

Africa is building.

What Ibrahim Traoré and his allies are doing is nothing short of revolutionary. They are tearing up the old playbook, pushing back against centuries of foreign domination, and laying the groundwork for a continent that governs itself, feeds itself, educates itself, and defines its own destiny.

This is what Pan-Africanism looks like in the 21st century.

It's not just a flag. It's not just a slogan. It's steel, sweat, concrete, and code. It's borders being blurred by trains instead of wars. It's African youth seeing leaders who look like them and speak with clarity about their future.

I believe in this future.

And that is why, to me, Ibrahim Traoré is **The Architect of New Africa.**

Closing Reflection

As I close this chapter, I'm reminded that revolution isn't just an act—it's a mindset. It's a decision to see beyond the borders drawn by colonizers, beyond the stereotypes fed to us by foreign media, and beyond the limitations others have placed on what Black nations—and Black people—can achieve.

Captain Ibrahim Traoré embodies that revolutionary mindset. Whether history will ultimately deem him a liberator or a controversial figure remains to be seen, but one thing is certain: he has reawakened a Pan-African imagination that has long been suppressed. He's reminded us that Africa is not the world's charity case—it is the world's cradle, and quite possibly, its future.

This chapter isn't just about Burkina Faso. It's about us—all of us in the African Diaspora—asking ourselves where we stand. Are we still waiting for permission, or are we ready to take ownership of our stories, our economies, and our futures?

We cannot afford to be passive observers. Whether we're in Baltimore or Bamako, Harlem or Harare, Atlanta or Accra—our fates are intertwined. We must support African sovereignty not out of nostalgia or symbolism, but because our global liberation depends on it.

Pan-Africanism in this era is not romanticism—it's strategy. It's practical. It's digital. It's infrastructural. It's generational.

I wrote this chapter not just as a journalist, but as a son of Africa, a student of struggle, and a believer in Black power across continents. The road ahead won't be easy. It never has been. But if Traoré and his allies are laying tracks—then we, too, must lay foundations: in our schools, our businesses, our politics, and our consciousness.

Let's be clear: the world is watching.

But more importantly, our children are watching.

Let them see us rise.

Chapter 24

The Power We Carry: From Toussaint to Tomorrow

When we know our power—when we truly grasp the divine gifts the good Lord placed within us before we ever drew breath—and when we begin to value ourselves in a world that has tried to kill us, demonize us, mislabel us, and extract from us while giving nothing back, then and only then do we begin to win. When we take that pain and turn it into purpose, that trauma and channel it into creativity, we reclaim our narrative. We become unstoppable.

Victory begins when we tell our own stories about our own heroes. Toussaint L'Ouverture in Haiti. Thomas Sankara in Burkina Faso. Zumbi in Brazil. Nanny in Jamaica. Nat Turner in the United States. These are names our children deserve to know— not just Martin and maybe Malcolm, but the full tapestry of Black brilliance and bravery across the globe.

Our young people must learn about Little Willie Adams right here in Baltimore, a businessman who built a Black financial empire when the odds said he shouldn't even try. They must know about Reginald F. Lewis, who came straight out of East Baltimore to make world history with the $985 million takeover of TLC Beatrice. And Annie Turnbo Malone—long before Madam C.J. Walker—who created not just a product line for Black women's hair, but an entire industry supported and powered by us, training generations of beauty professionals through the colleges she built.

These stories aren't in our schoolbooks. Instead, children are still told that Christopher Columbus "discovered" America. But we now know better. We know that Africans arrived in the Americas long before 1492. That Mansa Musa, the richest king in human history, ruled from Mali and sent 1,000 ships westward across the Atlantic. That the Olmec heads of Mexico bear the clear imprint of African presence. This is not myth—it is fact. And as these deeper truths come to light, our self-worth rises with them.

That's why education—real education—is sacred to me. It's not just about literacy; it's about legacy. It's about political power, too. Most of us aren't taught about the Black Reconstruction legislators who helped rebuild this country after the Civil War. But they were there. And if they could achieve all they did under terror and repression, imagine what we can do now.

We must convert this knowledge into power. That begins with knowing our gifts, using our talents, and aligning them with a tribe that shares our values. That's the role of the entrepreneur—not just to build wealth, but to build community. To connect, collaborate, and create.

And above all, to *reach back*.

The greatest responsibility of success is not the shine—it's the service. To whom much is given, much is required. This mindset must flow from one generation to the next without hesitation. Each one must teach one. Each one must lift one.

"You cannot carry out fundamental change without a certain amount of madness. It comes from nonconformity, the courage to turn your back on the old formulas, the courage to invent the future."
— *Thomas Sankara*

That's why we do this work. That's why BMORENews exists. That's why we recognize over 2,900 Black entrepreneurs through the Joe Manns

Black Wall Street Awards across the country. That's why we build platforms that tell our stories. It's not for vanity. It's for vision.

So now we ask:
What legacy will you build?
Who will you lift up next?
What truth will you teach that schools won't?

Because the future of Black empowerment isn't coming—it's already here.
And it's waiting on *you*.

Closing Reflection:

This is more than a conclusion—it's a call to action.

If the previous chapters were about reclaiming history, this one is about creating it. It's about understanding that the power we seek is already within us, placed there by God, shaped by struggle, and sharpened by generations who dared to dream beyond their circumstances.

The future of Black empowerment isn't abstract. It's tangible. It's in our businesses, our classrooms, our barbershops, our pulpits, our podcasts, and our platforms. It lives in the stories we choose to tell—and those we refuse to let die. It grows every time we teach our children the names left out of their textbooks and every time we choose purpose over profit, principle over popularity.

This chapter reminds us that legacy isn't built in monuments—it's built in people. In how we invest, how we educate, how we serve, and how we love our own. Empowerment isn't a slogan—it's a system. It's policy, it's practice, it's partnership.

To honor those who came before us, we must do more than remember—we must *build*. Brick by brick. Business by business. Truth by truth.

Because the next Sankara, the next Nanny, the next Reginald F. Lewis might be sitting in a classroom right now—or reading these words, wondering if their voice matters.

It does. **You** do.

So the final message is simple: This isn't the end.

It's the handoff.

CHAPTER 25

QUIET GIANTS

Greatness, real greatness, is not flashy. It doesn't need a spotlight or a press release. It shows up humbly, consistently, and in service to others.

I'll never forget when Magic Johnson came to Baltimore around 2003 with the Greater Baltimore Urban League. He was promoting financial literacy and entrepreneurship — but what stood out most to me wasn't the business talk. It was how he stopped to greet everyone. Every single person. Magic didn't act like a superstar. He acted like a brother. That's greatness.

Back in '95, Muhammad Ali visited Coppin State University. No bodyguards. No handlers. Just The Greatest, standing among us like one of us. I watched in awe as he embraced every person at that reception. He didn't just shake hands — he *connected*. That was a moment etched in my soul.

Then there's Charles "Choo" Smith, my brother and a Baltimore icon. He doesn't have Magic's height or Ali's global fame, but make no mistake:

Choo is a giant. He's spent decades building youth empowerment programs, launching his national "Communiversity" movement with support from Ray Lewis. I've seen him work tirelessly for over 15 years, always focused, always thinking ahead. Despite all he's accomplished and the stars he's met, Choo remains the same cool, grounded man. His goal is simple: get us to work together, leave the ego behind, and uplift our people.

Ron Busby is cut from the same cloth. A national business leader who built a multimillion-dollar enterprise and now serves as President of the U.S. Black Chambers, Inc. I've run into him at the White House and even across the country in Portland, Oregon — and every time, he's been approachable, present, and purposeful. That's what happens when you're walking in your purpose. Greatness follows.

And let me tell you about Mayor Marion Barry. No matter how busy he was, he always took my calls — even when I was just a young journalist. He didn't have to. But he did. That's what made him great: he saw people, not positions.

The late Raymond V. Haysbert, Sr. — the Dean of Business — was the same way. Though he was already a member of the prestigious Presidents' Roundtable, a network of Black millionaires, he still found time to help local entrepreneurs. He helped launch the Greater Baltimore Black Chamber of Commerce and mentored countless business owners. He was my very first advertiser. That's legacy in motion.

Al Hutchinson belongs on that same list. As the outgoing CEO of Visit Baltimore, Al has been a steady and visionary presence in the city. He's been the face of hospitality and tourism in Baltimore, not only elevating the industry but doing so with deep integrity and purpose. Now, as he prepares to embark on a new chapter—launching a firm with his wife—his work continues in a new form. His decision is a testament to the courage it takes to bet on yourself and to build something legacy-driven. Al's leadership calls to mind another tourism pioneer, Carroll Armstrong, who also helped shape Baltimore's image decades ago. Like Carroll, Al understands that promoting a city is about more than hotel nights and conference bookings—it's about pride, narrative, and equity. He made sure Baltimore's story included all of us. That, too, is what greatness looks like.

This is what greatness looks like.
It's not boastful. It's not arrogant. It's quiet strength, disciplined service, and radical humility. It shows up early, stays late, and brings others along.

As the late Shirley Chisholm said, "Service is the rent we pay for living." I pray to stay humble no matter what I accomplish. Kipling's *If* reminds us of the power "to walk with kings—nor lose the common touch." That line resonates deeply.

From Baltimore to Burkina Faso, from boardrooms to barbershops, we need to return to that mindset. We need to unlearn individualism and re-embrace communalism — where the village matters more than the spotlight, where success is measured by how many we bring with us.

This is our ancestral rhythm. It's in our DNA. And now, it's time to remember who we are.

In the Boot Prints of Giants

I've always loved war movies—starting with the old westerns featuring cowboys and Indians. Even as a child, I found myself rooting for the Indigenous people. Something in me, even at five years old, empathized with their struggle. Later in life, I learned from my father that his grandmother, Mollie Morton, was Blackfoot. He used to say she could "carry a bucket of water on her head and one in each hand—and never spill a drop." That image stuck with me. Grace under pressure. Strength in motion.

My father was a soldier. He served in Korea. My mother's father, Joaquin Calderon, gave his life in service as a member of the U.S. Coast Guard. One of my earliest Halloween costumes was as a U.S. Marine. At the time, I had no idea about Montford Point—the segregated training ground for the first Black Marines. But I've since learned what that legacy meant. I'm not a soldier, but I was raised by one. And I was shaped by many.

War, as brutal and painful as it is, remains part of the human experience. And those who answer that call—who put on the uniform and stand in harm's way—are heroes. Whether they fought for the flag, for family, for freedom, or for the person beside them, their courage commands respect.

Over the years, mentors like "Tiger" Davis—a veteran and Maryland state legislator—taught me a great deal about what military service means in the Black community. My father did, too. They opened my eyes to stories that don't make the history books: stories of bravery, sacrifice, and deep injustice. They taught me about General Daniel "Chappie" James Jr., the legendary fighter pilot who became the first African American four-star general in U.S. history. His ascension in 1975 shattered ceilings and expanded the collective vision of what was possible.

I've come to understand that the freedoms we now enjoy—education, careers, even the opportunity to build businesses—are gifts earned by those who wore the uniform. We often take these blessings for granted. But there are millions across the globe who may never know such liberty. Tiger often reminds me that families like mine—Black families—are direct beneficiaries of that sacrifice.

He also made sure I understood this: with every war, Black soldiers pushed the line forward—inch by inch, despite the weight of racism. They served with valor, yet came home to face lynch mobs, job discrimination, and systemic exclusion. Still, their service laid a foundation for broader progress— inside the military and far beyond it.

Consider the "Six Triple Eight"—the 6888th Central Postal Directory Battalion—the only all-Black, all-female unit deployed overseas in World War II. Tasked with clearing a massive backlog of mail under near-impossible conditions, they did it with unmatched precision and resolve. Their excellence quietly challenged the assumptions of both race and gender in America's war effort.

From the Revolutionary War to Afghanistan, Black soldiers have fought not only for a nation—but for dignity, representation, and future generations. James Forten, a veteran of the Revolutionary War, returned to become a prominent businessman and abolitionist. Many others followed suit—serving, surviving, and then *leading*. They became entrepreneurs, educators, political figures, and spiritual anchors in their communities.

My father's friends were among them. Haysbert, a Tuskegee Airman. Dr. Calvin Jenkins, president of Coppin State University and a proud veteran. General Larry Ellis, a four-star general, a Morgan State alum, and a personal mentor. He literally watched me grow up—and stood on stage as I accepted my master's degree in Journalism. That moment held a weight beyond the degree. It represented the full arc: from sacrifice to scholarship, from service to storytelling.

Black military history is American history. From the mostly Black First Rhode Island Regiment—who helped tilt the Revolutionary War—to the Buffalo Soldiers, whose bravery helped "win the West," our people have always been at the front lines. The 761st Tank Battalion—the "Black Panthers" of World War II—proved their valor under General George S. Patton in critical campaigns like the Battle of the Bulge. Their performance in battle earned the respect of peers and commanders alike, and they carved their names into history with steel, grit, and fire.

These are not just stories. They are living testaments to resilience, legacy, and purpose.

We owe these veterans more than a day. We owe them our vigilance, our gratitude, and our drive to build upon what they made possible. As we fight for economic and political power today, we walk in the boot prints of those who fought before us—on battlefields both abroad and at home.

Closing Reflection

Greatness is quiet. It doesn't shout or seek the spotlight—it shows up humbly, consistently, and in service to others. True greatness isn't about fame or fortune; it's about the depth of one's commitment to lifting others and building community.

From Magic Johnson's connection with everyday people to Muhammad Ali's warmth, and from Charles "Choo" Smith to Raymond Haysbert, greatness comes in many forms—but always carries the same core: radical humility, purposeful service, and relentless dedication.

It is never individualistic. Greatness is communal, rooted in legacy and accountable to future generations. Our Black military heroes—from the Revolutionary War through World War II and beyond—embody this truth. Their sacrifice and resilience are woven into our DNA. They gave us freedom, dignity, and the opportunity to keep pushing forward.

We stand on their shoulders. And so, we must remember: greatness is walking with kings without losing the common touch. It is service as the rent we pay for living. It means showing up early, staying late, and bringing others along for the journey.

Greatness isn't measured in awards—it's measured in how the village thrives. It's about collective progress, not personal glory.

The future of Black empowerment depends on this understanding. We must embody quiet strength, disciplined service, and radical humility. That is the blueprint for greatness.

As we reflect on the quiet giants who shaped our communities—not with noise, but with purpose—we must also recognize that greatness evolves. Sometimes, it wears a suit and stands behind a podium. Sometimes, it governs counties or rises to the U.S. Senate.

Legacy isn't built only in back rooms and barbershops—it's shaped in chambers of power. And today, in Prince George's County, one of the most compelling examples of that evolution is underway. From civic service to national leadership, the rise of Black political power in "Gorgeous Prince George's" isn't just historic—it's blueprint-worthy.

CHAPTER 26

THE PRINCE GEORGE'S POWER SURGE

Over the past half-century, Prince George's County has transformed from a suburban stronghold into one of the most powerful Black political centers in America. Once home to just a single Black state senator, it now boasts a bench of seasoned, strategic, and barrier-breaking leaders—none more impactful than three extraordinary Black women: U.S. Senator Angela Alsobrooks, County Executive Aisha Braveboy, and Maryland First Lady Dawn Flythe Moore. Their rise signals more than personal achievement—it represents a new era of Black political authority rooted in service, strategy, and sisterhood. Together, they are not only reshaping Maryland; they are redrawing the contours of what Black leadership in America looks like.

And I've watched it unfold with pride. When I think of "Gorgeous Prince George's," I don't just see names and titles—I see a remarkable arc of transformation. From a time when a single Black senator was a novelty, to today's reality of a thriving, Black-led political powerhouse, the journey is nothing short of historic. Especially when viewed through the lens of its synergy with Baltimore, it becomes clear: the twin engines of Black political power in Maryland are stronger—and more aligned—than ever.

This evolution didn't happen overnight. In 2002, Republican Michael Steele made history as Maryland's first Black statewide elected official, serving as Lieutenant Governor. Long before that, in 1974, Tommie Broadwater, Jr. became the first Black state senator elected from outside of Baltimore City, representing Prince George's County. He served until 1983, and his rise marked the beginning of a generational shift.

Together, Baltimore City and Prince George's represent the twin engines of Black political power in Maryland. Their collective influence is undeniable—and it's growing.

In 2002, Republican Michael Steele made history as Maryland's first Black statewide elected official, serving as Lieutenant Governor. Long before that, in 1974, Tommie Broadwater, Jr. became the first Black state senator elected from outside of Baltimore City, representing Prince George's

County. He served until 1983. His rise marked the beginning of a shift.

Former state Senator Clarence Mitchell III once told me that when Broadwater entered the legislature, the Baltimore delegation—then just 11 Black members—played a crucial role in mentoring and supporting him. Despite their small numbers, those Baltimore lawmakers were highly effective. Mitchell's point was clear: with what is now the largest Black caucus in America, Maryland should have the strongest, most visible, and most impactful Black Agenda in the nation.

That foundation laid decades ago has since blossomed. Consider Dereck E. Davis, who served the 25th District in the Maryland House of Delegates from 1995 to 2021. Or the late Senator Ulysses Currie, who began his legislative service in 1987 and spent more than three decades representing District 25. And Senator C. Anthony Muse, a pastor and veteran public servant, returned to the Maryland Senate in 2023 after earlier terms in both chambers.

The turning point came in November 1994, when Wayne K. Curry was elected as Prince George's first Black County Executive. He served two terms and set the tone for the future—opening the door for a generation of Black leadership.

From one senator to a bench of power players, Prince George's County has become a symbol of what's possible. And when its influence is combined with Baltimore's, the potential for real, lasting policy change is immense.

The Three Black Queens of Prince George's County Politics

Prince George's County has long been fertile ground for Black political excellence. But in recent years, its story has been shaped—and elevated—by three remarkable women. These Black queens have not only broken barriers, they've redefined leadership in ways that impact the entire state of Maryland and beyond.

Angela Alsobrooks: From Prosecutor to U.S. Senator

Angela Alsobrooks, a proud Maryland native, made history in 2024 when she was elected to the United States Senate. Her journey to the upper chamber of Congress wasn't just a personal achievement—it was a milestone for the entire state, as she became the first Black person elected to the U.S. Senate from Maryland.

Angela's guiding light has always been the lesson passed down from her great-grandmother: to get off the sidelines, go farther, and do better. After graduating from Duke University and the University of Maryland School of Law, she began her legal career clerking in local courts before becoming the first full-time Assistant State's Attorney handling domestic violence cases in Prince George's County.

She quickly rose through the ranks, making history as the youngest and first woman elected as the County's State's Attorney. Under her leadership, violent crime dropped by 50%. In 2018, she was elected County Executive, where she prioritized economic growth and job creation, becoming one of Maryland's top job creators within two years.

While I haven't spent much time with Angela personally, I've watched her rise closely. Her U.S. Senate victory over David Trone, despite his $6 million war chest, was nothing short of political mastery. With Larry Gibson by her side and a grassroots movement behind her, Alsobrooks ran a textbook campaign rooted in strategy, authenticity, and community. Her victory was not only a personal triumph—it was a win for Black women across Maryland and a beacon for little Black girls everywhere.

Aisha Braveboy: A Servant-Leader with Vision and Grit

In June 2025, Aisha Braveboy was elected County Executive in a special election, becoming a historic figure in Prince George's County governance. Her win came after six years as State's Attorney, where she built a reputation as both a fierce prosecutor and a compassionate public servant.

I've known Braveboy since her days in the Maryland House of Delegates. She has always been about the work—grounded, focused, and principled. In her final days as State's Attorney, she secured a first-degree murder conviction while simultaneously preparing to take office as County Executive. She wasted no time addressing major issues, swiftly organizing support for a new Police Chief and uniting stakeholders behind an Interim Superintendent for Prince George's County Public Schools.

What sets Braveboy apart is her rare experience in all three branches of government: Legislative,

Judicial, and Executive. She's not new to this—she's true to this. From managing a $24 million budget and leading over 200 staff members, to spearheading legislative reform and championing community health initiatives, Braveboy brings a depth and breadth of service that's hard to match.

During the mortgage crisis, she offered pro bono help to homeowners. At Children's National, she fought for hospitalized youth. And as State's Attorney, she prioritized public safety while expanding programs that addressed the root causes of crime.

Braveboy's leadership style is bold yet collaborative. She isn't chasing headlines—she's delivering results. She's the kind of leader who understands the bridge between Baltimore and Prince George's County because she's walked it for years.

Both Alsobrooks and Braveboy share a prosecutorial background, but unlike others—say, former U.S. Vice President Kamala Harris—they successfully transitioned into executive roles. That matters. In a country where 5% of the world's population accounts for 25% of the incarcerated, and where nearly 40% of U.S. prisoners are Black men, Black communities have a complicated relationship with prosecutors. A prosecutor alone won't win Black hearts. A servant-leader with a track record of tangible impact will. And both these women have earned that respect.

Dawn Flythe Moore: The Strategist Behind the Power

The third queen is someone I've known the longest—**Dawn Flythe Moore**, First Lady of Maryland. Don't let the ceremonial title fool you—Dawn is one of the sharpest political minds in the state.

She tried to advise Kathleen Kennedy-Townsend during her failed 2002 gubernatorial bid. Later, she was an architect behind Anthony Brown and Martin O'Malley's 2006 victory, which led Brown to become the state's first Black Democratic Lieutenant Governor—and ultimately helped pave his path to becoming Maryland's first Black Attorney General.

Today, as the First Lady, Dawn Flythe Moore is arguably Maryland's own Michelle Obama. She brings experience, wisdom, and fearlessness. I've seen her on the ground in the streets of Baltimore, especially during the 2015 Freddie Gray Unrest.

She didn't play it safe—she showed up. From Shake-n-Bake on Historic Pennsylvania Avenue to the Western District station to Park Heights, home of Pimlico Racetrack, she was present in our most trying moments.

She understands Maryland politics down to its molecular level. And she leads with grace, grit, and a commitment to the community. Her support of Governor Wes Moore isn't just marital—it's strategic, spiritual, and political. In a nation where 70% of Black families are led by women, seeing a strong, unified Black family in leadership is more than refreshing—it's revolutionary.

If there is a second Black President of the United States, don't be surprised if his last name is Moore. Dawn Flythe Moore is doing the work to help make that vision real. And what's especially important to me: she understands the vital role of supporting the Black Press.

Reflection

What's happening in Prince George's County is more than a local success story—it's a model for what Black political power can look like when it's rooted in community, shaped by experience, and guided by vision. The rise of Angela Alsobrooks,

Aisha Braveboy, and Dawn Flythe Moore reminds us that leadership isn't about titles—it's about impact. Each of these women has taken their seat at the table, not just to be present, but to shift the direction of the conversation and the course of policy.

Their journeys also prove a deeper truth: that Black excellence, when nurtured and supported, becomes unstoppable. These leaders didn't emerge overnight. They stand on the shoulders of generations—of Tommie Broadwater, Clarence Mitchell III, Ulysses Currie, Wayne Curry, and so many more—who laid the foundation and dared to demand more for Black Marylanders.

But what makes this moment in Prince George's County historic is not just who is in office. It's what they represent. These women symbolize a new Black political paradigm—one that is bold, unapologetically service-driven, and deeply attuned to the needs of our people. And in a time when the nation continues to wrestle with inequality, injustice, and the erasure of truth, their presence is proof that the Black Blueprint is alive, thriving, and evolving.

This is not just their chapter—it is ours. And it is far from finished.

As these powerful women shape policy and influence lives, another battlefield demands equal attention: who gets to tell our stories. Political power means little without narrative power. If we don't own the lens through which the world sees us, we risk being misunderstood—or erased altogether.

That's why Black media ownership is not just a business move—it's a survival strategy.

CHAPTER 27

THE POWER OF BLACK MEDIA OWNERSHIP: SUPPORT BLACK MEDIA!

No matter how popular you are or how high your ratings climb, corporate America has a quick trigger finger when it comes to Black broadcasters. What many people don't see—or choose not to acknowledge—is the quiet, ongoing battle behind the bright lights of national television. To the public, the on-air personality is a star. Behind the scenes, however, they often walk a razor-thin line just to stay in the spotlight.

From the outside, the industry looks glamorous. But behind closed doors, it's often exhausting and filled with contradictions. Black professionals in media are constantly navigating a duality—too Black for some audiences, not Black enough for others. The same dynamic plays out for Black police officers, service members, and executives in predominantly white institutions. This balancing act is relentless.

W.E.B. Du Bois captured this internal conflict in *The Souls of Black Folk*:

"It is a peculiar sensation, this double-consciousness... One ever feels his two-ness—an American, a Negro; two souls, two thoughts, two unreconciled strivings... whose dogged strength alone keeps it from being torn asunder."

That's the tightrope we walk. We want to speak our truth and honor the communities that shaped us—but we must also operate within the limits imposed by the networks. And when those networks are NBC, ABC, CBS, CNN, or MSNBC, the truth is simple: it's not our house. We're guests. And guests don't get to move the furniture.

That's why **ownership** matters. That's why **control** matters.

As Billie Holiday famously sang, "God bless the child that's got his own." Many of us came to this realization not by choice—but by **necessity**.

Roland Martin is a powerful example of what happens when Black journalists take control of their own platforms. For decades, Martin worked in traditional media—print, radio, and TV—at outlets like *The Fort Worth Star-Telegram*, CNN, TV One, and *The Tom Joyner Morning Show*. But it wasn't until he launched **Roland Martin Unfiltered**, his own digital news network, that he took full control of the **narrative**.

When TV One canceled *News One Now* in 2017, Martin didn't back down—he **doubled down**. He built a daily digital news show broadcast on **YouTube, Facebook, and podcast platforms**, funded entirely by his own team. Today, *Roland Martin Unfiltered* has more than **1.8 million YouTube subscribers** and over **26,000 videos**. He now delivers news without **corporate interference**—informing, challenging, and advocating on his own terms. His model shows that **Black media ownership** can be both **sustainable** and **transformative**.

Don Lemon has also stepped into independent territory. After being fired from CNN in April 2023 amid falling ratings and internal drama, he quickly pivoted. In early 2024, Lemon launched **The Don Lemon Show**, initially slated to debut on **X (formerly Twitter)**, with Elon Musk as his first guest. After taping, Musk pulled the plug. Lemon responded by releasing the episode on **YouTube and podcast platforms** instead. It was a **turning point**. Rather than be silenced, Lemon went directly to his audience. He now commands over

714,000 YouTube subscribers and **1.3 million Instagram followers**, joining a growing movement of Black journalists reclaiming their **voice** through digital media.

And then, of course, there's **Oprah Winfrey**—the most iconic example of Black media ownership. From humble beginnings in rural Mississippi, she rose to become the **"Queen of Media."** *The Oprah Winfrey Show* ran for **25 years** and redefined how media connects with audiences. But beyond the screen, her savvy business acumen led her to create **Harpo Productions** and the **Oprah Winfrey Network (OWN)**—a platform dedicated to stories created by and for **Black audiences**.

Oprah didn't just succeed—she **redefined success**. Her influence spans **literature, wellness, spirituality, politics, and philanthropy**. Her endorsement of Barack Obama in 2008 was a **political game-changer**. With awards like the **Presidential Medal of Freedom**, Oprah's legacy is about more than wealth—it's about **impact, access, and power**. Just ask Maryland Governor **Wes Moore**, who credits her support as pivotal to his journey.

Byron Allen: Fighting for Economic Justice in Black Media Ownership

While **Oprah Winfrey** exemplifies the power of **media influence, Byron Allen** represents the fight to dismantle **economic barriers** that **Black-owned media** face. In **June 2025**, Allen settled a groundbreaking **$10 billion racial discrimination lawsuit** against **McDonald's**. The case revealed a tiered "**African American**" **ad-buying system** that placed Black-targeted media in a separate category with significantly **smaller advertising budgets** than the **general market spend**. This **discriminatory practice** limited the ability of **Black-owned outlets** to grow and sustain themselves **financially**.

Byron Allen's company, **Allen Media Group**, started more than **30 years ago** with a single talk show and has since grown into a **media powerhouse** owning assets like **The Weather Channel, The Grio, HBCU GO**, and numerous **local TV stations**. His legal battles with giants such as **Comcast** and **DirecTV** further exposed how **systemic exclusion** in **advertising spend** has stifled Black media's **economic power**.

This settlement not only signals **renewed commitment** from major corporations to invest **equitably** in Black media but also highlights that **ownership** is about more than **content control**—it's about securing the **financial resources** to sustain and expand **Black voices** in an evolving **digital landscape**.

But the story of Black media ownership runs far deeper than today's icons. It traces back centuries—from Sierra Leone to Haiti to New York City in the early 1800s—when the first Black newspapers emerged to cover our community the way white-owned media never would. The names are chiseled in my soul: **Sam Cornish, John Russwurm, John Murphy, Robert Sengstacke Abbott, Claude Albert Barnett, Ida B. Wells, Ethel Payne**—all the way up to people like **Dorothy Brunson**, the first Black woman to own a radio station, right here in my hometown of Baltimore, and the inimitable **Catherine Liggins Hughes**.

Cathy Hughes is a trailblazing media mogul, entrepreneur, and the founder of **Urban One** (formerly Radio One), the **largest African-American-owned broadcasting company in the nation. As of 2024, her estimated personal net worth is around **$250 million**, built through decades of leadership in radio, television, and digital media. Her company was listed as **#9 on the BET 100 in 2015**, with a corporate net worth of **$450.8 million**.

Hughes launched Radio One in 1980 with a single station in Washington, D.C., and grew it into a multimedia empire that includes **over 50 radio stations**, **TV One**—a cable network she launched in 2004—and a suite of digital platforms catering to Black audiences. Her wealth stems from executive leadership, stock ownership, media investments, speaking engagements, book deals, and appearances.

Known for her resilience, Cathy once lived at her station to save it during hard times. But through vision and sheer determination, she built an empire that not only generates wealth but **amplifies Black voices and culture**. Her story is not just one of financial success—it's a legacy of **empowerment, impact, and ownership** in an industry that rarely makes space for Black leadership.

These pioneers didn't just **inform** the community— they **empowered** it.

And that brings us to **film**.

I'll never forget my first Media Arts class at Coppin State with Professor Ronn Nichols. I was excited to study broadcast production—but quickly learned why Black media voices matter.

As Wendell Phillips said in *Narrative of the Life of Frederick Douglass*, "The story of the hunt must be told by the hunted." That's why we need filmmakers like **Oscar Micheaux**, who made 44 films at a time when no other Black man was doing so. He opened the door for legends like **Spike Lee** and **Ryan Coogler**.

Black Panther, directed by Coogler, became the highest-grossing film ever with a majority Black cast—raking in $1.3 billion, winning Oscars, and earning Marvel's first Best Picture nomination. That's not just a win at the box office—it's a **cultural revolution**.

But Hollywood still prefers slave narratives. Try making a film about **Toussaint L'Ouverture** or the **Haitian Revolution**—you won't find a blockbuster budget waiting. Stories about Black resilience and triumph are still rare, especially ones that center strong Black men, intact Black families, or real Black heroes.

We need more films that reflect our full reality—not just singing, dancing, or cracking jokes, but leading surgeries, commanding courtrooms, innovating in labs, and building skylines. The images we consume shape how we see ourselves. If we want stronger Black communities, we must see ourselves in our full brilliance. But if we're content with weaker ones, then keep feeding on a mainstream narrative that was never built for us to thrive—only to fit in.

Today, social media is the new television. But many of us are treating it like it has no consequences. We need to reclaim our digital image and raise the standard. Everything ain't for everybody. And what we post today can shape how the world sees us tomorrow.

That's the power—and the responsibility—of Black media ownership.

Conclusion: The Mic is Ours Now

We are no longer asking for permission to tell our stories. We are building the platforms, owning the cameras, running the presses, and programming the airwaves. From the street corners of Tulsa to the studios of Atlanta, from Baltimore to the Bay, Black media is no longer just a reflection of the culture—it *is* the culture.

This is not just about having a voice; it's about owning the microphone.

To be seen, heard, and respected on our terms requires more than talent—it demands ownership. Because when we own, we're not just telling stories—we're shaping destinies, challenging systems, and rewriting the narrative in real time.

So, whether you're behind a camera, holding a mic, running a newsroom, producing a podcast, or funding Black media from the boardroom, know this:

The power is in our hands. Let's not just use it— let's protect it, build with it, and pass it on. Support Black Media!

Closing Reflection

The journey toward true empowerment in Black media ownership is more than a fight for airtime or headlines—it is a movement to reclaim our stories, our identities, and our futures. Every platform built, every story told by us and for us, chips away at centuries of silence and misrepresentation. It reminds us that our voices are not just echoes in someone else's house, but the foundation of our own.

As we move forward, we carry the legacy of those who dared to own the narrative when the odds were stacked against them. Their courage lights the path for new generations to not only speak but to shape culture, policy, and power. Ownership is not just about controlling media—it is about controlling destiny.

In this moment, we are the architects of our narrative landscape. The mic is ours, the stage is set, and the time is now. Let us hold fast to the responsibility and the privilege of that power, building platforms that uplift, challenge, and inspire. Because when we own the story, we own the future.

CHAPTER 28

WHAT I WOULD SAY TO MY YOUNGER SELF

Believe in yourself. Know that God has given you everything you need to succeed. Each of us is born with unique gifts and talents — no one else on Earth has exactly what you have. There is not another *you* anywhere on the planet. It's your job to nurture those abilities, to harness the power within, and to direct it toward positive, constructive action. Nourish your mind, body, and soul.

It is through passion that we discover purpose — and through purpose that we find peace.

Use the insights from this book to expand your thinking. Don't be limited by what you see — tap into what you imagine. Dream. Think big. The only real limitations are the ones we place on ourselves. With a determined mind, nothing and no one can stop you.

Life will throw distractions your way. You'll face disappointments and moments that try to knock you off your path. If you fall, get back on your horse and keep riding. Judge Maybelean once said, "If you keep walking, you can get through anything." I take that advice literally, every day I'm blessed to breathe God's air.

Be grateful. Gratitude is understanding that every breath, every step, every moment — even something as routine as a car ride — is a miracle to someone who's paralyzed or in a coma. We take too much for granted. At any moment, your world can be turned upside down.

Surround Yourself Wisely

You are the company you keep. Surround yourself with people who are going somewhere — even if they're halfway across the world. In today's world, you can build a community of like-minded people online. But also be present where you are. Know how to put the phone down — even off — to recharge your peace.

Learn how to engage with people face-to-face. It's an art. If you want a friend, be a friend. If you want love, give love. If you want respect, offer respect. And always remember: sometimes, you'll need to draw boundaries. Life has its clowns — don't be one of them. Maintain your dignity and self-respect.

If you want to be an engineer, surround yourself with the brightest engineers. If you want to excel in any field, seek out the best mentors you can find. And listen. I'll admit — I've been a poor listener. So, I take notes. I record. I do whatever I can to retain what's being taught. You should too.

Financial Wisdom

Now, let's talk about credit — something too many learn about the hard way. Treasure your credit score. Don't buy things on credit unless it's absolutely necessary. And if you do, pay it back on time. America is built on debt traps. Don't fall into one because of your own lack of discipline.

Live below your means. Don't try to impress anyone. Pay your bills. Credit affects your business, your relationships, and your family. And while you're managing debt wisely, also save and invest. Build multiple streams of income. Multiply your gifts and talents — don't waste them. Don't let them fester unused.

As I often say: *What Jamal does most, Jamal does best.* In other words: repetition creates mastery. Build good habits. Build healthy relationships. Treat people how you want to be treated — because we get back what we give.

Avoid bad habits. Avoid bad company. Your life depends on it.

Mental and Emotional Health

Pray like it's up to God, but move like it's up to you. And please — stay mentally healthy.

I always recommend having a therapist. And if your therapist doesn't have a therapist, find a new one. Ideally, find a grounded Black therapist — someone who understands the unique pressures and micro-traumas of being Black in America. A good therapist helps you process, reflect, and grow. They help you unpack the stress, replay events, and plan for better responses next time.

Love and Relationships

To my younger self — be more selective in the women you choose to share your life with. A woman can be one of the greatest blessings in a man's life. But with that blessing comes responsibility. Be mindful of what you do and how you do it.

Again — prayer.

CHAPTER 29

PASS THE BALL

This may ruffle some feathers, but the truth doesn't need permission. I've seen the same dysfunction everywhere — from prestigious universities to national Black organizations, from nonprofits to youth sports leagues.

We don't pass the ball.
We don't pass the baton.
We don't hand off the mic. We don't share the torch. We build powerful institutions — churches, media platforms, nonprofits — only to treat them like personal property, as if they exist to serve one figurehead. One ego. One gatekeeper who refuses to let anyone else dribble.

And when we do pass the ball, it's often in crisis — a scandal, a collapse, a forced resignation. That's when we suddenly "consider succession." And too often, the pass is made to a family member, not the most qualified or most prepared — just someone who shares the last name.

So, I have to ask: Is it your organization, or is it ours?

In cities like mine, there are more nonprofits than corner stores. But many founders start them without understanding how they actually work. You might think you're the CEO for life — but your board can vote you out tomorrow. That's how it's supposed to work. That's governance. That's sustainability.

And yet, we clutch the title like it's an heirloom. We sit on boards until the rapture, refusing to groom a successor, refusing to mentor the next generation, refusing to step aside — even when it's long past time.

Why?

Maybe because we've built our whole identity around these roles. Maybe because we fear irrelevance without the title. Maybe it's ego. Maybe it's fear. But here's what it definitely is: shortsighted. And harmful.

Young people are watching. And make no mistake — they see what's happening. They see our refusal to share power, and they draw the obvious conclusion: "The elders aren't going to let us in."

So, they start their own organizations. And who can blame them?

We haven't welcomed them.
We haven't trained them.
We haven't poured into them.

Instead, we point fingers. We criticize from a distance. We dismiss their language, their fashion, their platforms. We shake our heads and call them "lost." But what we really are — is in the way.

And it's our fault.

We have created a generation of brilliant, visionary young leaders who don't want to deal with us — because we've given them every reason not to. We didn't make space. We didn't extend grace. We didn't lead by example.

Leadership is not a crown — it's a relay. Not a possession — but a responsibility. And if you're holding the baton past your leg of the race, you're slowing down the whole team.

So, if you've been sitting in the same seat for twenty years and still have no idea who's coming behind you, ask yourself why. If your only answer is, "They don't listen," maybe it's time to show them something worth following. Young people don't follow advice — they follow example.

So please, with all due respect to your decades of service and sacrifice:
Pass the damn ball.
Let the next Jordan run the play. Let the next leader shine.

The team can't win if you never let anyone else touch the rock. Because if the blueprint ends with you, it was never a blueprint at all.

CHAPTER 30

THE BUILDERS — BALTIMORE'S BLACK ARCHITECTS OF POWER

Power is never given. If you want it, you have to take it. And after you take it, you have to be able to manage it, like Senator Corey McCray in East Baltimore, the founder of the BEST Democratic Club. Baltimore's legacy of Black power was built by determined visionaries who refused to wait for permission to lead. Together, they shaped not only this city but the nation. To separate their stories would be to misunderstand the very foundation of our progress.

Long before the Civil War, Baltimore was home to the largest free Black population in America. Positioned just south of the Mason-Dixon Line, the city has always stood at the crossroads of oppression and opportunity. Despite systemic hostility, Baltimore has long been a stronghold of Black excellence—a proving ground where Black leaders dared to defy limitations and build enduring legacies.

These are the stories of Baltimore's architects of power—individuals who didn't just walk through doors, but built them, often under threat, scrutiny, and attack. Each made deliberate, strategic, and visionary moves in hostile territory. Together, they form what we call the Black Blueprint.

Isaac Myers (1835–1891): The Trade Union Pioneer and Cooperative Visionary

Born a free Black man in a slave state, Isaac Myers carved a path few dared to tread. Denied public education, he attended a private day school run by Rev. John Fortie. At 16, he began work as a caulker—sealing seams on ships—in Baltimore's bustling harbor.

The post-Civil War era brought harsh competition for jobs, with over 1,000 Black caulkers forcibly displaced due to white worker strikes. Undeterred, Myers proposed a bold solution: workers pooling resources to build a cooperative shipyard and railway. The Chesapeake Marine Railway and Dry Dock Company, founded in 1866, was a pioneering effort employing over 300 Black workers at its peak.

Myers's leadership extended to labor organizing as president of the Colored Caulkers Trade Union Society and then as the first president of the Colored National Labor Union in 1869—a vital organization challenging the era's entrenched racial exclusions in labor.

Beyond labor, Myers was deeply involved in civic life, serving as Baltimore's first known African American postal inspector under President Ulysses S. Grant's administration. He also founded and led several key institutions, including the Maryland Colored State Industrial Fair Association, Colored Business Men's Association of Baltimore, and the Colored Building and Loan Association.

Isaac Myers's legacy is a testament to resilience and ingenuity. He showed how cooperative economics and organized labor could build collective Black power—and that vision still resonates today.

Thomas R. Smith (1871–1938): From Enslavement's Shadow to Business Powerhouse

Before "Little Willie" Adams made his mark, Thomas R. Smith had already crafted his legacy in stone—and mahogany. Born in Calvert County,

Maryland, to a mother who had been enslaved and a father who died fighting in the Civil War, Smith moved to Baltimore and built one of the most significant Black-owned businesses in America.

In 1912, he opened Smith's Hotel at Druid Hill Avenue and Paca Street. At its peak, it was the largest African-American hotel in the country — lavishly appointed with marble, mahogany, and red carpet. Smith's Hotel became more than a place to stay; it was a cultural and economic hub for Black elites and traveling performers, a rare space of dignity amid Jim Crow segregation.

By his death in 1938, Smith had amassed an estate worth more than $120,000 (millions today), largely through real estate. He was a philanthropist, a political power broker, and a visionary. Smith's legacy proves that even in an era of exclusion, Black excellence could build and thrive.

George W. F. McMechen (1872–1961): The Legal Mind That Dismantled Segregation

Yale-educated and Morgan College's first graduate, George McMechen made history not just in the courtroom but in his choice of address. When he moved his family into a white neighborhood in 1910, their presence triggered Baltimore's first residential segregation ordinance—and the nation's.

Instead of backing down, McMechen partnered with fellow attorney William Ashbie Hawkins to challenge it. Their legal resistance helped set the stage for *Buchanan v. Warley* (1917), where the U.S. Supreme Court ruled that race-based housing laws were unconstitutional.

McMechen's bravery and brilliance created ripples across the nation. Every integrated neighborhood owes part of its freedom to the steps he took in West Baltimore.

Lillie May Carroll Jackson (1889–1975): The Mother of Freedom

Lillie May Carroll Jackson is rightly known as the "Mother of Freedom." For 35 years, she led the Baltimore NAACP branch—transforming it into one of the most effective in the country. Before the Civil Rights Movement had a name, Jackson had a blueprint. She championed nonviolent protest long before it became a national strategy, insisting that dignity was non-negotiable.

One of her most impactful campaigns was the "Buy Where You Can Work" movement, launched in the 1930s. At a time when Black Baltimoreans were consumers but rarely employees, Jackson led boycotts that forced white-owned businesses to open their doors to Black workers. These economic justice tactics were revolutionary, laying the groundwork for later national movements.

Under her leadership, Baltimore's NAACP became a powerhouse of legal, political, and grassroots action. She recruited lawyers, trained youth, and organized voters. She also helped fund and support a young Thurgood Marshall. Her legacy lives not just in laws changed—but in a generation emboldened to fight for their rights.

Enolia Pettigen McMillan (1904–2006)
Educator. Activist. Architect of Power.
Enolia Pettigen McMillan broke barriers as the first woman to lead the NAACP nationally, but her impact on Baltimore and the broader Black freedom struggle runs far deeper. Born to a formerly enslaved father, McMillan moved to Maryland as a child in pursuit of educational

opportunity. She graduated from Howard University in 1926 and later earned her master's from Columbia University—where her groundbreaking thesis exposed the racial inequities in Maryland's segregated school system.

As a teacher, principal, and president of the Maryland State Colored Teachers' Association, she fought for equal pay, fair curricula, and desegregation in public education. After retiring in 1968, she defeated Juanita Jackson Mitchell to become president of the Baltimore NAACP, leading the local branch through a financial crisis and raising the largest local contribution to save the national office from bankruptcy.

In 1984, she became national president of the NAACP, helping move its headquarters to Baltimore and amplifying its advocacy against apartheid, economic injustice, and the Reagan administration's civil rights rollbacks. McMillan also made history as the first woman to chair the Board of Regents at Morgan State University.

A lifelong fighter for equity in education, civil rights, and Black leadership, Enolia McMillan's century-long legacy helped lay the foundation for

Black power in both Baltimore and the nation. A street near the NAACP's Baltimore branch now bears her name—a fitting tribute to a woman who never stopped building.

Juanita Jackson Mitchell (1913–1992): The Legal Trailblazer Who Advised Presidents
Juanita Jackson Mitchell didn't just follow in her mother's footsteps—she blazed her own path across the legal and political landscape. In 1950, she became the first Black woman to practice law in Maryland, graduating from the University of Maryland Law School. But her impact had already begun.

At just 18, Juanita founded the City-Wide Young People's Forum, a powerful youth mobilization initiative that united West Baltimore churches in activism, lectures, and cultural events. In 1938, she married Clarence M. Mitchell Jr., forming one of the most influential civil rights power couples in the country.

As legal counsel for the NAACP, she fought and won key desegregation cases, often working with Thurgood Marshall. Her victories helped integrate schools, public accommodations, and workplaces across Maryland. She organized massive voter registration drives and advised both Presidents Kennedy and Johnson on civil rights. She stood at the intersection of grassroots power and national policy—and never flinched.

William "Little Willie" Adams (1914–2011): From Numbers to Nation-Builder

Little Willie Adams came to Baltimore as a teenager and started as a numbers runner. But he didn't stop there. With sharp instincts and bold strategy, Adams became a mogul, a philanthropist, and a political kingmaker.

He co-founded the Parks Sausage Company, the first Black-owned business to go public, and helped establish the Super Pride grocery chain. He invested in local businesses, backed politicians, and fought for desegregated golf courses. When federal authorities tried to criminalize him, the U.S. Supreme Court overturned his conviction.

His wealth was never just about accumulation—it was about transformation. His foundation and investments fueled the economic engine of Black Baltimore for decades.

Dorothy Brunson (1939–2011): Media Pioneer
Dorothy Brunson was the first Black woman in the nation to own a radio station, and she did it right here in Baltimore. From her base in Walbrook Junction at WEBB Radio, she not only broke into an exclusive industry—she redefined it.

Brunson eventually expanded into television, purchasing and operating stations in multiple cities. She used media not just to entertain, but to empower, putting stories of Black life, Black business, and Black struggle into the public sphere with dignity and control.

Reginald F. Lewis (1942–1993): Billion-Dollar Visionary
Reginald F. Lewis didn't just break glass ceilings—he shattered economic gravity. A Harvard Law grad and former Wall Street lawyer, Lewis completed the first billion-dollar leveraged buyout of a global company by a Black American when he purchased Beatrice International in 1987.

He believed in legacy. He founded the Reginald F.

Lewis International Law Center at Harvard, and dreamed of a museum to honor Black Marylanders—now a reality at Baltimore's Reginald F. Lewis Museum.

He once said, "Keep going, no matter what." That motto defined his life—and it defines the road ahead.

Donna S. Stevenson (Contemporary): Building a Digital Future for Economic Justice
In today's digital economy, Donna S. Stevenson is among the most important builders of Black power. As co-founder and CEO of Early Morning Software, Inc., she leads the team behind PRISMCompliance.com—the nation's most advanced platform for Supplier Diversity and Economic Inclusion.

Under her leadership, PRISM helps clients manage billions of dollars in contracts and payments, audit payrolls by race and gender, and enforce compliance in DEI programs from HUD to DOT. It was the first-to-market software to automate market availability and set M/WBE contract goals based on real-time data—a revolution in inclusion.

But Donna's impact goes far beyond technology. She consults mayors, advises C-suite executives, and has lectured around the world—from South Africa to the UK. She founded the COMPASS Institute for Diversity, Equity & Inclusion, and helped form the National Leadership Team for Economic Inclusion in the COVID-19 Economy.

Her awards include Maryland Top 100 Women, Black Caucus Entrepreneur of the Year, and US DOT Woman-Owned Business of the Year. Through her work, Donna proves that software, policy, and justice are not separate pursuits— they're part of the same fight.

Wanda Queen Draper
Wanda Queen Draper is a Baltimore-born journalist, media executive, and cultural leader whose career has spanned decades of public service, community impact, and institutional leadership. A graduate of the University of Maryland School of Journalism, with further studies at Johns Hopkins and the University of Maryland School of Law, Draper has left her mark across Baltimore's media and civic landscapes.

She spent 25 years at WBAL-TV, serving as Vice President of Programming and Public Affairs, and also held roles at WJZ-TV, Maryland Public Television, and the Baltimore News American. Beyond journalism, she led community engagement and operations at the National Aquarium and trained at elite institutions like the Disney Institute.

Draper's most visible contribution is to the Reginald F. Lewis Museum of Maryland African American History and Culture. She served on its founding board, helping raise $40 million for its creation and permanent exhibits, and later returned as Executive Director, where she continues to elevate African American heritage and civic consciousness.

A champion of education, hunger relief, and housing, Draper views community service as a lifelong obligation. She serves on numerous boards and mentors rising leaders like Jimmy Britton of Class Act Catering. Married to Dr. Robert Draper, she is the proud mother of two and grandmother of four.

Wanda Draper stands as a true builder—an architect of institutions, opportunity, and impact.

Joseph "Joey" Brown III — The Final Innovator

Joseph "Joey" Brown III didn't just inherit the family business — he revolutionized it.

In a city where tradition often defines the funeral industry, Joey Brown dared to lead with innovation, compassion, and a commitment to the future. As the owner and operator of Joseph H. Brown Jr. Funeral Home, he modernized the way Baltimore handles end-of-life care — making history by building the only crematory in Baltimore City, and introducing alkaline hydrolysis, also known as water cremation — one of the most eco-friendly disposition methods available today.

"For a greener, cleaner, kinder, gentler cremation service."

That's not just a slogan. It's a philosophy.
Water cremation — or alkaline hydrolysis — uses water, heat, and an alkaline solution to gently accelerate the natural decomposition process. Sometimes called aquamation, green cremation, or resomation, it's not only flameless but dramatically reduces carbon emissions and energy consumption

compared to traditional flame cremation.

While the rest of the country slowly adapts to shifting preferences, Joey positioned Baltimore ahead of the curve. According to the Cremation Association of North America (CANA), 56% of Americans chose cremation in 2020, more than double the rate from two decades ago. By 2040, four out of five Americans may choose cremation. Joey saw this coming — and built infrastructure to meet it.

But Joey didn't stop with technology. He reimagined the experience of saying goodbye. His team places deep emphasis on ceremony, healing, and personalization — because honoring a life isn't just about logistics; it's about legacy. Whether through private family gatherings, public community memorials, or eco-conscious memorialization, Joey's vision is rooted in service and sensitivity.

"Ceremony brings hope and enlightenment."

That's the ethos behind every service — to light the path forward for families navigating loss. From offering guidance on cremation caskets, to customized memorial urns, to keepsakes that hold ashes or flower petals, Joey's operation reflects not only tradition but transformation. He respects the past while preparing families for the future — spiritually, emotionally, and environmentally.

In a city rich with history and challenged by change, Joey Brown built more than a crematory. He built trust. He built relevance. He built options. And in doing so, he honored the sacred duty of laying our loved ones to rest with dignity and grace.

Joseph "Joey" Brown III is not just a funeral director. He is a builder — reshaping how Baltimore commemorates life, one family at a time.

Legacy of the Blueprint
These architects—Myers, Smith, McMechen, Jackson, Mitchell, Adams, Brunson, Lewis, and Stevenson—stood on no one's shoulders but God's and each other's. They were not accessories to someone else's history. They authored their own chapters, built their own doors, and set the terms of their own legacies.
They did the unthinkable. They built the

impossible. They gave voice to the voiceless, vision to the unseen, and structure to dreams that the world told them could not stand.

They laid bricks with blistered hands, wrote laws with sharpened minds, created jobs out of thin air, and birthed movements from the marrow of their convictions. In boardrooms, in courtrooms, in classrooms, in backrooms—they moved mountains.

And they left us more than stories. They left us blueprints—divine, deliberate, time-tested paths for building Black power with excellence, courage, and faith.

Because if God gives you the vision, He will provide the provision. But the labor is still ours.

To every young person in Baltimore—listen closely:
You are not a statistic.
You are not a stereotype.
You are not the sum of someone else's low expectations.
You come from builders. You come from brilliance.
You come from Black greatness that did not just survive—it soared.

This is not just history. This is a summons. A playbook. A charge.

You hold the hammer now. Will you settle for mediocrity, or will you aim for the same excellence as did our ancestors? Will you go the unforgiving mile to help or feed someone like Harriet Tubman, or are you too busy being distracted on less productive activities?

This is the Black Blueprint. And it's your turn to build. Together, these visionaries did more than succeed—they laid blueprints for us to follow.

Author's Note on Chapter 32: Why Grace Matters

As we approach the final chapters of *Black Blueprint*, I want to pause and speak directly to you, the reader.

This chapter may feel different from the others — less about policy, business, or media strategy, and more about the *inner work* required to lead, to build, and to sustain progress.

But make no mistake: **grace, mercy, emotional intelligence, and forgiveness are not extras — they're essentials.**

Movements collapse when ego overtakes purpose. Coalitions fall apart when offense goes unforgiven. Families and neighborhoods fracture when we don't make space for each other's growth.

This chapter is about that space.

It's about the deep, quiet work that doesn't get televised: learning to love ourselves, release what's heavy, and see each other with clearer eyes. It's about becoming the kind of people who can carry the vision forward — *not just loudly, but wisely.*

If you've come this far in the book, you've done the strategic thinking. Now let's do the soul work. Because *we can't build a new world with wounded hearts.*

Let's keep going — together.

— Doni Glover

CHAPTER 31

THE GRACE WE MUST GIVE MERCY, MEDIA, AND THE MISSION

At the heart of any real movement is not just strategy or ideology — it's relationships. If, as political strategist Vernon Jordan once said, *"There are no permanent friends, no permanent enemies, only permanent interests,"* then navigating those interests requires more than sharp tactics. It requires grace. Mercy. Emotional intelligence.

Grace is getting what we don't deserve. How many times have we found ourselves spared from situations that could've gone terribly wrong?

Mercy is not getting what we do deserve. How often have we been blessed — even when we weren't doing what we were supposed to? Some of us did the opposite of what was right, and still, God showed us favor.

Both grace and mercy demand humility. And both are essential when working across lines of difference, history, and ego. We can't change yesterday, but we can learn from it. In fact, we must — because those who don't learn the lesson are doomed to repeat the class. Individually, community-wide, worldwide: it's all the same.

Emotional intelligence is the ability to recognize, understand, manage, and influence emotions — both your own and others'. It often matters more than intellect when it comes to leading people, resolving conflict, building coalitions, or earning trust. Without it, power becomes fragile. With it, power becomes sustainable. At its core, emotional intelligence is rooted in one thing: *respect*.

Politics is a brutal game — the dirtiest, some say. Corporations, lobbyists, and politicians play for keeps. It's the arena where power is negotiated and decisions are made about who gets what, when, and where — and who gets left with the scraps. It's not just about laws or elections. It's about the pie — and who's cutting it.

From West Africa's Sahel to West Baltimore's Sandtown, Black communities across the globe are engaged in political and economic fights that demand evolved leadership. Leadership that understands history, yes — but also one that can hold space for nuance, disagreement, and growth.

Because sometimes, the people we most need to build with are the same ones we've never trusted — or never met.

Sometimes, there's painful history. Sometimes, it's just a lack of connection. But the question remains: *Can we sit down? Can we talk? Can we listen? And more importantly, can we do it with respect?*

To even begin such a conversation, we need a shared understanding — of who we are, where we've come from, and how we got here. I must know my journey. You must know yours. And then we must honor each other's paths. Without that mutual respect, there can be no unity. Just noise. Ego and emotion take the wheel, and before we know it, we're arguing over turf while others are trading resources.

And let's be real — a lot of the distrust among us isn't natural. It's programmed.

American media has long misrepresented Black people. From Tarzan swinging through Africa like its savior, to the whitewashed version of the Lone Ranger — who was actually inspired by Bass Reeves, a Black U.S. Marshal — we've been fed lies from childhood. Hollywood, the news, and now even social media often portray Blackness as poor, violent, hypersexual, and underdeveloped.

We are praised for our rhythm, but ignored for our reasoning. Society celebrates our swag, our dunking, our sprinting, our impossible moves. They cheer for us on the field, at the mic, on stage — even, grudgingly, on the tennis court and golf green. But when it comes to the boardroom, the lab, the Supreme Court, or the rooms at NASA — the tone shifts. The access narrows. The imagery changes.

Worse still, some of us internalize that shift.

We start believing that proximity to whiteness, wealth, or "respectability" means we've arrived. We cut ties with the communities that raised us. We stop going to PTA meetings, NAACP meetings, Urban League gatherings, or even our family cookouts. We become obsessed with being accepted by people who don't care two shillings about us.

And that's exactly how the cycle continues.

We must stop seeking permission to be ourselves: **Unapologetically Black!** We must put that energy into becoming *okay with who we are* — not the version the media has painted, not the version white supremacy allows in small doses, but our full, healed, whole selves.

We have to accept ourselves. Love ourselves. Without validation from anyone else. We have to confront our trauma, name it, heal it — and from that healing, grow our self-respect.

On Forgiveness

But even as we work to heal and grow, one of the hardest steps in that journey is this: **forgiveness**.

Forgiveness doesn't mean forgetting. It doesn't mean ignoring the hurt. It doesn't mean we stay silent when wronged. What it means is *choosing* to release the weight of bitterness — *without malice or ill will*.

When people hurt us — especially after we asked them not to, after we trusted them — it is deeply human to want revenge. We want them to feel what we felt. We want *payback*. The big payback.

But **hurt people hurt people — until they are healed**. And forgiveness is a part of that healing. Not for them — but for *us*. It does more for the forgiver than it ever does for the trespasser.

We say, "Forgive us our trespasses, as we forgive those who trespass against us." We beg God for grace, for mercy, for forgiveness — and yet we so often struggle to extend that same gift to others.

I have to check myself all the time:
Did I give grace? Did I offer mercy? Did I forgive? Did I operate from a position of love?

Because before we can truly forgive anyone else — we must start with **ourselves**. Say it: **I forgive myself!** *Now, walk in that forgiveness!*

Have we forgiven ourselves for the time we wasted goofing off? For the moments when we played small? For the harm we caused others — and ourselves — out of fear, or ego, or pride?

Until we forgive ourselves, it's hard to walk forward in love. But when we do — when we give ourselves grace, extend mercy, and embrace forgiveness — we begin to show up differently. Stronger. Softer. Wiser.

And *that* is how transformation begins.

That's why grace is revolutionary.

When we meet each other with mercy — when we pause, breathe, and recognize the invisible weight that so many of us carry — we shift the dynamic. We build bridges where there were only walls. We reclaim our narrative and step closer to collective power.

Grace isn't weakness. It's wisdom.

As we chart a path forward — in business, in politics, in media — let us remember: the real mission is not just to win, but to *win together*. And that starts with giving each other the space to grow, to be seen, and to be understood.

That's how we move forward.

Together.

Reflection: Giving Grace, Building Power

1. **When** have I let ego or old wounds block me from building necessary relationships?

2. **Who** in my life or community do I need to extend grace to — not for them, but for the sake of the mission?

3. **What** media messages have shaped my views of other Black people — consciously or unconsciously?

4. **How** can I grow my emotional intelligence as a leader, organizer, or entrepreneur?

5. **Am I willing** to sit at the table with those I once saw as adversaries if it means progress for our people?

Final Thought:
What would it look like if grace became our strategy, and love became our leverage?

CHAPTER 32

We Are the Blueprint

"Because if the blueprint ends with you, it was never a blueprint at all."

Some said I wasn't supposed to make it this far.
But I always knew better.
Because I was raised by people who didn't just hope — they knew.
They knew what was in me before I ever fully saw it in myself.
They knew that greatness doesn't come from circumstance — it comes from conviction.
What my parents planted in me didn't just survive — it grew. It blossomed into a mission.
And that mission stretched far beyond North Avenue.

I once thought success meant proving the world wrong.
Now I know: real success is proving our ancestors right.
They weren't building for applause.
They were building for us.

With limited tools but unlimited vision, they laid a foundation rooted in faith, strategy, and love. Whether they were running corner stores in Sandtown or kingdoms in Ethiopia, the message was the same:
We have everything we need.

Black Media Is a Movement

I've walked through City Hall and through villages on the other side of the world. I've been called a journalist, a businessman, a grandfather, a friend — and I've worn each title with pride.
But at my core, I am still that boy from North Avenue — East and West — carrying a blueprint etched in survival, vision, and truth.
This isn't just a memoir. It's a roadmap.
A reminder:

That Black Wall Street isn't a myth or a memory — it's a movement.
That legacy isn't about what we leave behind — it's about what we build now.
That power isn't given — it's *cultivated*.
From the barbershop to the ballot box.
From the pulpit to the pressroom.

From West Baltimore to West Africa.
We are the infrastructure we've been waiting for.

That's why we must support and harness Black-owned media — *BMORENews.com* and *BlackUSA.News*.
These aren't just news outlets — they're connective tissue. They tell our stories authentically, foster local economies, and amplify our voices where it matters most.

We Are Not Divided

A man recently said to me, *"We don't stick together like other races do."*
Number one, it is dangerous to compare oneself, one's community, one's country to another because you haven't walked in their shoes.
Number two, too often we as Black Americans think everything is peachy with other ethnic groups. Jerks come in all flavors.
There are Koreans who hate other Koreans and Nigerians and Frenchmen who hate their own.
I also told him that we are only 15% of the population.
Despite everything being thrown at us — including the kitchen sink — we consistently

dominate any and every field we are able to penetrate.
I told him I've never been more proud to be Black. In light of all of the obstacles hurled at us every day of the year, Coco Gauff still wins the French Open, and David Steward still runs the largest Black-owned company in America. I'll take it.

For the record:
The largest Black-owned company in the U.S. today is World Wide Technology (WWT), a global IT solutions provider based in St. Louis.
Founded in 1990 by David Steward, WWT generates approximately **$17–20 billion in annual revenue** and employs around **10,000 people worldwide**.

Please miss me with the defeatist talk.

Writing this book was critical to me because if I've heard it once, I've heard it a thousand times: "Black people just don't stick together."
I am sick and tired of hearing us say that — because it's not entirely true.
And to the extent that it is, there are reasons — reasons that stretch all the way back to the plantation.

We were terrorized. Raped. Murdered. Enslaved. Divided by force.

Our children sold. Our bodies exploited. Our identities stripped.

Escaped Africans were hanged as warnings. Our women were forced to breastfeed the children of our captors.

In New Orleans, executed insurrectionists had their heads placed on spikes.

We have survived the Tuskegee experiment.

Mass sterilizations in North Carolina.

The terrorism of the Ku Klux Klan.

Bombs in Tulsa.

Another in Philly.

Let alone the stress from just being Black in America on a day-to-day basis.

And yet we are still here.

Still rising. Still building. Still thriving.

Given the scope of this trauma — compounded by redlining, segregation, poor schools, and broken promises like the Homestead Act and G.I. Bill — I say this with my whole heart:

Black America deserves a standing ovation from the world.

And we must never forget places like **Mound Bayou, Mississippi** — founded in 1887 by freedmen like Isaiah T. Montgomery.

This wasn't just a town — it was an empire of excellence.

With its own hospitals, banks, and schools, Mound Bayou was the Black blueprint long before hashtags and headlines.

Legacy and Grandchildren

I've been called "the plug." "The great connector." Maybe.
But I know this: Black people cannot afford to be divided.
Whether I'm in an Uber with a Nigerian driver or a church in East Baltimore, I'm always looking to bridge the gaps — because I know the distance between East and West Baltimore is no different than the distance between African Americans and our brothers and sisters on the continent.

Mainstream media has poisoned the well.
Before we meet, we've already been misinformed about each other.
That's why Black media matters.
And that's why **we must think like heads**, not tails.
We must teach our kids about **Mansa Musa**, the

pyramids, the **Zulu**, and the greatness that runs through our veins.

Lauryn Hill once wrote about "access."
I, too, want that for every Black child: access to education, opportunity, self-love — and global awareness.

Economic Power and Collective Duty

Let's be clear: nearly **$2 trillion** flows through Black hands in America every year. That's a global economy. Did you hear me? Arguably the 10th largest economy on earth!
If we even directed a *fraction* of that toward Black-owned businesses and media, we could transform our communities overnight.

You don't have to like me to support Black business.
And I don't have to like you.
But if I'm creating jobs for people who look like you, don't block the blessing.
If you are creating Black jobs, it is my innate obligation — due to good ol' fashioned home training — to support you.

Supporting Black-led institutions is not a favor.
It's our collective duty.
And apparently, I'm pretty good at it — just ask the last four governors of Maryland.

Reprogramming the Narrative

The problem isn't just economic.
It's psychological.

If the only media we consume shows us as violent, criminal, or broken — then that's the image that gets baked into our subconscious.
Garbage in, garbage out.

But the flip side is just as true:
Nutrients in, nutrients out.

We are not just what we eat — we are what we read, watch, and repeat.
We have to flood our minds with information that heals, informs, and empowers.
We need media that reminds us who we are.

The Closing Charge

We are not victims.
We are victors!

Where others see problems, I see possibilities.
Where others give up, I dig in.
Like Malcolm and Martin before me — I will never give up on us.

If all you want to do is talk about what's broken in our community — don't talk to me.
We know what's wrong. We live it.
What we need is mass healing, self-love, Black therapy — and yes, White therapy too.

America must confront its original sin and make amends.
Reparations are not optional.
We don't need saving.
We need investment.
We don't need sympathy.
We need equity.

We are the blueprint — and it doesn't end with us.
It begins again, with every hand we reach back to lift.

You've read the blueprint.
Now go live it.

This is bigger than me.
It always has been.

That's why I asked my brother in Oakland to take us home.

Mic drop.

AFTERWORD

To me, this book is about bringing to light what so many people are still in the dark about. Too often, our communities are kept uninformed—especially when it comes to politics. That's where I focus first, because **tens of millions of dollars flow through our neighborhoods every year for things like education, job training, and housing.** But without access to the right information, we miss out.

That's why I started my show on *BlackUSA.News*—to shine a light. From the beginning, people were calling, wanting to come on the show. And they still are. I've had the chance to host key voices in Oakland politics—like **Kevin Jenkins, Pam Price, now-City Councilwoman Janani Ramachandran**, and I was proud to support **Barbara Lee for Mayor**. I've also interviewed **former mayors Elihu Harris and Sheng Thao**, among others. These conversations matter, because **real solutions come from real dialogue**.

In the Bay Area, like in so many Black communities across the country, **Black-owned businesses are struggling.** Our unions are no exception—

carpenter unions, for example, lack Black men in their ranks. Why are we not in those union halls? Why are we not being trained or hired in large numbers? These are systemic problems that don't get enough airtime.

That's why *BlackUSA.News* is so powerful. It's not just a local platform—it's a **national conversation**. What's happening on the East Coast is happening out here too. And if you're doing something out there that's working, we need to know about it. If we've got something working here, we want to share it. **This is how we learn from one another—how we build smarter, stronger, and more Black-friendly systems.**

We don't have the luxury of being disconnected. Because these aren't just East Coast issues or West Coast issues. These are **American problems**. Across the country, **Black entrepreneurs and communities are floundering—not because of lack of talent, but because of a lack of access, understanding, and political will.**

That's what makes Doni Glover's work so important. His **tenacity, energy, and vision** bring people together. He has a gift for identifying media voices—new talent who can help educate and elevate our people. He's created a platform that doesn't just inform—it mobilizes. And we need more of that.

Therefore, when you read *Black Blueprint*, don't just see it as one man's journey. See it as a roadmap—a call to connect, to build, and to move our people forward from Baltimore to Burkina Faso and everywhere in between.

— **Doug Blacksher**
Host, BlackUSA.News – Oakland, California

ACKNOWLEDGMENTS

I am profoundly grateful to the teachers and professors who challenged me to reach higher, from my earliest days in pre-K through graduate school. Their steadfast commitment to education and excellence helped shape the man I am today.

To my family, friends, mentors, and everyone who has walked alongside me on this journey—thank you for your unwavering support, invaluable lessons, and boundless love.

This book stands on the foundation you all helped build.

ABOUT THE AUTHOR

Donald "Doni" Glover is an award-winning journalist, entrepreneur, and community advocate from Baltimore. He is the founder of *BMORENews.com*, *BlackUSA.News*, and the Original Black Wall Street SERIES, and the host of the Emmy-nominated Doni Glover Show. Doni has dedicated his life to empowering Black communities through media, entrepreneurship, and education. A proud father, grandfather, scholar, and entrepreneur, Doni carries forward the legacy of resilience and excellence rooted in his Baltimore upbringing. This is his fourth book, a blueprint for collective strength and progress.

www.ingramcontent.com/pod-product-compliance
Lightning Source LLC
Chambersburg PA
CBHW071955070526
44583CB00015B/1206